# THE ANTHROPOLOGY OF MAGIC

# THE ANTHROPOLOGY OF MAGIC

Susan Greenwood

Oxford • New York

English edition
First published in 2009 by
**Berg**
Editorial offices:
First Floor, Angel Court, 81 St Clements Street, Oxford OX4 1AW, UK
175 Fifth Avenue, New York, NY 10010, USA

Berg is the imprint of Oxford International Publishers Ltd.

**Library of Congress Cataloging-in-Publication Data**

A catalogue record for this book is available from the Library of Congress.

**British Library Cataloging-in-Publication Data**

A catalogue record for this book is available from the British Library.

ISBN 978 1 84520 670 3 (Cloth)
978 1 84520 671 0 (Paper)

Typeset by Apex CoVantage, LLC, Madison, WI, USA
Printed in Great Britain by the MPG Books Group, Bodmin and King's Lynn

**www.bergpublishers.com**

# CONTENTS

For
Pat Caplan and Olivia Harris

# INTRODUCTION

The study of magic is central to the discipline of anthropology. Anthropologists have studied magic extensively, even when other social science disciplines have dismissed it as bizarre or peripheral, but it has not always been fully understood. Due to a scientific emphasis on reason, the actual experience of magic has often been reduced to terms and explanations alien to its processes. Many anthropological theories have implicit assumptions about the ultimate irrationality of magic or of the inferiority of magic when compared to science, or they reduce magic to its social or psychological effects, factors that can be understood more readily by the social sciences. But while magic is often explained precisely by what it is not, magic is at the heart of anthropology in terms of the issues it raises in relation to human experience, people's lived realities and the meaning of science. The time has come to propose another understanding of magic, and it is the aim of this book to examine magic as an aspect of human consciousness. I shall show how magic can affect everyday conceptions of reality, and how magic can be an analytical category as well as a valuable source of knowledge. Offering a window into human processes of mind, this perspective can illuminate our understandings of a whole range of situations—from traditional anthropological contexts of witch beliefs and shamanism to how we conduct science—as well as challenge our assumptions.

Studying the experience of magic calls for a different anthropological approach. When I first started my doctoral research in the 1990s, I made the decision to study magic from the inside, as a practitioner of magic as well as an anthropologist. I wanted to discover what could be learnt through direct experience. Over the years, I have explored various approaches to magic with Western magical practitioners, and I have participated in many witchcraft rituals, trained as a high magician, and worked with shamans. Each of these activities contributed to my realising the importance of examining an explicitly magical attitude of mind. I have used my experiences of direct insider research on magic as well as those of others to illustrate how this magical attitude of mind works as a research strategy in my two anthropological ethnographies: *Magic, Witchcraft and the Otherworld* (2000) and *The Nature of Magic* (2005).

The dual positions of working with the subjective experience of magic and also as a trained academic researcher not surprisingly resulted in some challenging issues of translation, as the languages of the directly experienced magical field and the more distanced stance of traditional academic research are on opposite ends of a spectrum. Sometimes they seemed mutually incompatible and mutually incomprehensible. So in trying to create a bridge of communication between the two, my anthropological role has been as a translator between very different worlds: the conventional academic sphere, which still seems to be heavily ideologically influenced by the Enlightenment ideals of reason and rationality, and the world of magic, a supposed realm of unreason. The two domains of academy and field were, for most of the period of my early research, quite distinct, with little communication between them. My research since has concentrated on the examination of the process of magic to try to bridge the gap, to make magic understandable, not only for anthropologists, but also for those who practice magic and for a more general audience beyond academia. This last, more general domain of the public was addressed in my writing *The Encyclopedia of Magic and Witchcraft* (2001, 2002, 2003; 2006).

In all of this work, I came to realise that despite varying and sometimes enormous cultural differences, there are also close similarities in the ways that people engage with the experience of magic—from such seeming extremes of so-called witchcraft, as practised in Africa,[1] to the recent European revival of witchcraft as a form of spirituality. And while much has been written about African witchcraft and magic, much less attention has been given to Western approaches. However, there is currently a tremendous surge of anthropological interest in magic in Western cultures, which is largely due to its use as an analytical category to elucidate a wide variety of processes and practices to do with modernity. *Magic* covers a repertoire of related terms and has versatility and plasticity; in the past, it has been used as a vague marker of otherness that freezes non-Western subjects in premodern time,[2] but it is now increasingly being employed as a counterpoint to liberal understandings of modernity's rational progress.[3]

Magic is also highlighted in a detraditionalisation of mainstream religions, whereby people turn from more orthodox practices and explore the direct experience of alternative spiritualities such as versions of esoteric Judaism and Christianity as well as various forms of paganism. Some of these Western magical practices have developed out of a significant and sustained history. While less obviously visible than surviving magical traditions in small-scale societies worldwide, historically, since Christianity became the dominant religion, there has always been a partly hidden and fragmented presence of magic in Western societies as expressed in numerous folk beliefs and mythologies. The more formal expression of this dates from the Renaissance, when certain magicians were influenced by the *Corpus Hermetica*, a body of first- to third-century Greek texts, with strong Neoplatonic influences aimed at bringing the individual closer to deity.[4] Since that time, there has been a substratum of magicoreligious ideas, cosmologies and ontologies incorporating Rosicrucianism, Freemasonry, theosophy and liberal Catholicism.

The occult tradition has been expressed in many ways, from the romantic creations of so-called Celticity used in regional power confrontations against English nationalism—the most obvious example being the poet W. B. Yeats's political campaign that invoked an Irish nationalist Celtic spirituality—to J.R.R. Tolkien's *The Lord of the Rings* (which sold 150 million copies) and J. K. Rowling's Harry Potter books (with more than 400 million copies sold), serving as just two recent examples of best-selling books[5] on magic that have been turned into hugely popular films.

The Western magical tradition has been associated with the upper classes and political leaders of the time. Take for example Cosimo de'Medici, who employed the Renaissance magician Marsilio Ficino to translate the *Corpus Hermetica* from Greek into Latin; or Queen Elizabeth I, who relied on John Dee, her court astrologer and adviser. More recently, during the twentieth century, it was said that Nancy Reagan, wife of president Ronald Reagan, and Princess Diana consulted astrologers. Magic has also been taken up by the middle classes: a revival in the nineteenth-century Hermetic Order of the Golden Dawn by leading Rosicrucians and Freemasons provided much of the impetus for the development of modern witchcraft, synthesized from various elements of high magic in the 1940s. Modern witchcraft in the early days of the 1950s was a middle-class pursuit, broadening its appeal from the 1980s on. Druidry likewise changed its image from an eighteenth-century gentlemen's club to a nature religion, a form of spirituality based in the natural cycles and energies of the earth, allegedly open to all. Magic reached its most working-class expression in chaos magick, a derivative of chaos theory and punk rock. Incredibly, all share a magical world view that would be broadly understood in principle by those in non-Western magically oriented societies.

It is this commonality of magic as a cosmological world view that enables us to make the comparisons between what might, on the surface, seem to be completely different practices of magic. A recent anthropological example that demonstrates this approach has compared African witch-doctors with Western political spin-doctors, as employed by U.S. president Bill Clinton and U.K. prime minister Tony Blair to ensure their continued political success.[6] While the spin-doctors might not be consciously working with magic *per se*, they are using emotional processes of mind that work in a magical or occult (hidden) fashion. Magical processes of mind are fuelled through emotion. By connecting with the desires of the voting public, these politicians try to ensure their own popularity and the popularity of their political agendas.

This parallel between African and European practices has made some anthropologists uncomfortable because it goes against ingrained, and sometimes unquestioned, assumptions, namely, the conceptual oppositions of a rational Western science and an irrational magic of the other, the traditional area of anthropological attention. What this means is that we in the West think as magically as they do. This can be very disconcerting for some, but a focus on similarities of magic as a human proclivity is a challenge that can open up new horizons of understanding in anthropology. Magic is a universal aspect of human consciousness; it is inherent in the mind. Magic has been associated with backwardness and primitivism, a negative trope in constructions of the primitive other, and has been banned from progressive ethnographies; but now the concept is being recast in new and exciting ways. Having been concealed in the West under a cloak of rationality, it is therefore particularly relevant to study magic in Western societies. Magic is alive and well as an analytical category in a whole range of new ethnographies.[7]

The approach taken here focuses on *magical consciousness*, a term that I use to describe a mythopoetic, expanded aspect of awareness that can potentially be experienced by everyone; it is expressed in myriad varying situations and contexts, and it informs both the shaping of cosmological realities and individual behaviour as well as social structures. Magic is therefore fully a part of human life, even if it has been devalued, suppressed and driven underground so that it manifests in what might appear to be unexpected forms. Thus magical consciousness is an aspect of mind that occurs in a multiplicity of ways in varying individuals, cultural contexts and through time. Anthropologists have traditionally been very wary of operating at such macro levels as human consciousness, preferring instead to centre attention on cultural particulars.[8] Of course, these particulars are a vital and valuable aspect of the discipline that gives anthropology its characteristic methodology of participant observation, but my focus is also on the universal, an orientation towards what connects, rather than what divides, us human beings.

Including the larger picture has the advantage of breaking down old divisions between the West and the other. By bringing these two categories of understanding together, we bring our shared humanity into perspective, and this is important and relevant to today's globalizing world as well as to the evolving relevance of anthropology.[9] Concentrating on similarities, rather than differences, between people can break down social divisions and encourage communication between disparate groups. Magic is a topic that has to be understood and explained on both micro (individual experience) and macro (universal) levels. The positive value of this approach is that it makes us look at ourselves as well as others; it brings us together and makes connections between phenomena that perhaps, at first sight, do not seem to be connected.

For any transformation of anthropological understanding to occur, magic has to be recognized as a legitimate form of knowledge. As I have indicated previously, this is a challenging move. In Western rationalist cultural, history magic has been systematically marginalized. Magic has been seen to be trying to do what science does, but is failing because it is based on false premises. Social scientists have described magic in various derogatory ways. Edward Tylor, in *Primitive Culture* (1871), saw magic as 'the most pernicious delusion that ever vexed mankind', and James Frazer thought that magic was a 'pseudo-science'. According to American anthropologist A. L. Kroeber (1876–1960), magic was characteristic of 'retarded' cultures; magical beliefs occurred in 'advanced' cultures only among the socially disadvantaged, psychotic or mentally subnormal. For Austrian psychiatrist Sigmund Freud (1856–1939), there was a parallel between primitive magical beliefs and neurotic and infantile delusions, whereas the French sociologist Emile Durkheim (1858–1917) and his disciples in the *Année Sociologique* school viewed magic as a negative and private activity opposed to public religion.[10] Even at the turn of the twenty-first century, Henrietta More and Todd Sanders wrote in the introduction to their edited book on witchcraft in postcolonial Africa that 'at the dawn of the new millennium, newspapers advertise weekend "Psychic fayres" where gullible [British] audiences listen to tarot card readings and the voices of the dead'.[11] Somehow Europeans (but not Africans, presumably) can still be seen as gullible. When it comes to issues of magic, the rationalism (and racism) inherent in anthropological discourse needs to be recognised and avoided.

In mainstream religions, magic is not only wrong, but has been seen as an act against God; a magician is often defined as a person using charms or spells to threaten the omnipotence of divinity. In historical religious discourses, magic has been associated with the 'maliciously manipulative', and it 'connotes the dark and the alone'. This usage has a long tradition. The practice of the art of magic has included 'vanishings, changes of shape, stature, and sex, transformations into other creatures (usually horrible), night visions and flyings (often on curious vehicles), the raising storms, the scattering of thunderbolts, the transporting of crops and cattle, the exciting and extinguishing of love, abortions, the inflicting of injury and death'.[12] Increasingly, magic was represented by the word *maleficium*. Magic was viewed as real and threatening: it was always potentially evil and potentially uncontainable.

The word *magic* comes from ancient Persia—the Magi were a class of priests—and the Greeks turned the word into *mageia*, later becoming *magia* in Latin. Both *mageia* and *magia* had negative associations that still exist today.[13] A dictionary definition of *magic* reflects this general negativity when it describes magic as 'the pretended art of influencing [the] course of events by occult [hidden] control of nature or of spirits, witchcraft; *black, white, natural*, - (involving invocation of devils, angels, no personal spirit); inexplicable or remarkable influence producing surprising results'.[14] So magic is a pretended art that produces results that are both surprising and cannot be explained.

Magic is an art that stems from a universal process of mind that has been systematically undermined and undervalued in Western cultures. Western cultural understandings have influenced the way in which Westerners view magic, and we therefore often find it difficult to write about magical experiences. Take for example the case of Richard Mabey, a naturalist, television producer, author of *Flora Brittanica* and a columnist for an English national wildlife magazine; someone not given to flights of fantasy or ventures into the irrational. Mabey is a self-confessed materialist, yet he has had a profound magical experience that he finds difficult to communicate within his usual categories of understanding.[15] On one particular May night, he describes listening to nightingales in Suffolk, England, as 'something close to a moment of communion':

> The setting was narcotic. A full moon, mounds of cow parsley glowing like suspended balls of mist, the fen arching like a lustrous whaleback across the whole span of the southern horizon. The nightingale was a shaman, experienced, rhetorical, insistent. I sank into its charms, a willing initiate. A shooting star arced over the bush in which it was singing. As I edged closer, its song seemed to become solid, to be doing odd things to the light. I was aware that my peripheral vision was closing down, and that I had no sense of where I was in space. And then, for just a few seconds, the bird was in my head and it was me that was singing.[16]

The shaman took Mabey to another place, another experience, something deep within himself. As someone who does not believe in 'the supernatural', Mabey finds this experience difficult to explain. He feels the nightingale in his head as a shaman, and he has what are usual physiological effects of a change in consciousness—his peripheral vision closing down, combined with a sense of body disorientation—but this is not understandable through science because it is 'more-than science'. His experience cannot be called religion either because he has had a 'spiritual communion' with a bird, rather than a deity, and this does not fall into the usual category of religion. Mabey says he often fudges his answer when asked about his spirituality because it is assumed that someone who looks at nature with 'more-than-scientific eyes' must believe in something behind that 'more-than'. Consequently, he avoids such difficulties of explanation.

Mabey's description of how the nightingale sang through him does not fit neatly into common definitions of science or religion. However his communion is an example of magical consciousness, the sort of experience that anyone can have through empathising deeply with another creature in the imagination, so much that bodily boundaries and distinct notions of self are temporarily abandoned. This is something that shamans in varying cultures would be familiar with—the metamorphosis of bodily awareness is a common feature of such magical transformations. Something similar happened to me the first time I tried a shamanic journey, a type of meditation whereby the imagination is used to explore the deep processes of the mind guided by the rhythm of a drumbeat.[17] The occasion was a workshop at a conference on the performing arts and shamanism in Cardiff, Wales, and all the participants of the workshop were instructed to find a hole in the ground and imagine themselves down into it. The aim of the journey was to find a spirit guide.

I remembered a dream I had had previously in which I was climbing down a deep tunnel in the middle of the earth, and it came back to me as I lay on the floor. It was tight and dark, a labyrinth of connecting, warrenlike tunnels which became tighter and darker and darker. I felt the pressure of the earth on and all around me. I could not breathe and I was paralysed by fear—too frightened to go on and too frightened to stop. I had experienced vertigo as a child, and it reminded me of this. Nevertheless, I knew that I had to go on, and as I crawled, the tunnel got tighter and tighter and I lost my skin—it was stripped off me, like a snake's. I felt myself come to an opening in the tunnel, a round space. I felt freer and found myself swimming in water in the round opening, but I felt the need to go on. This time the tunnel was narrow, but I could swim, and it seemed to be a straight line. As I swam, I felt the rest of me disintegrate and slip away, until I reached another space—an opening. I stopped and looked down on myself. I was a pile of bones. My bones were being picked over by a large, black crow. As I approached it, looking for its meaning, to my surprise, it turned into a large, white snow owl, and she let me nestle in her warm feathers and we tried to fly. We hopped around my bones, flying for a few wing beats, until we took off into the sky. At that time I had had enough, and my awareness returned fully to my body, lying on the floor of the workshop.

This experience had a profound effect on me, and I started to realize the power and importance of the imaginal experience in the whole process of magic. As an alternative mode of consciousness, magic can take a person via her imagination deep within herself and also, paradoxically, out into a wider emotional relationship with another being such as a nightingale or an owl—so much so that bodily boundaries appear to merge. I felt as though I had become the bird; I *smelt* her warm smell, and the smell took me into the experience of flight—I could *feel* the pull of the air on my wing feathers. I understood the experience as a spiritual communication with this bird.

Examining magic as such an intense experience is very challenging for the discipline of anthropology. The problem is that emotional and imaginative experiences associated with such shape-shifting cannot be understood purely by studying them by conventional scientific methods of analysis. The characteristic methodology of science, developed during the seventeenth century, has proved to be a rational benchmark by which anthropology has judged itself. The scientific method is a procedure performed in a laboratory to test a highly specific hypothesis within an accredited theoretical framework,[18] and 'it is precisely this "experimental method" which allows scientists today to lay claim to their immense cognitive authority'.[19] In the seventeenth century, the practical, experimental aspects of magic had contributed to part of the development of early science; they became absorbed into science, leaving other features of magic to be denounced as irrational. Indeed, a number of historians of science have 'refused to accept that something which they see as so irrational could have had any impact whatsoever upon the supremely rational pursuit of science'; their arguments 'seem to be based on mere prejudice, or on a failure to understand the richness and complexity of the magical tradition'.[20]

As magic cannot be fully understood from within the parameters of the experimental method, anthropologists, as social scientists, have developed a unique methodology of 'participant observation' with the people who they study. This methodology is far removed from the experimental laboratory, but nevertheless the scientific method still remains as something of an ideal—in theory, if not in practice—and anthropological theories do not easily account for experiences such as the owl shape-shifting I have described. Despite different approaches, some of which are more sympathetic than others, much anthropological debate has been 'an attempt to deal with the dilemma of how to interpret other people's' insistence that gods, demons and spirits exist.[21] Magic speaks to realms other than material reality. These realms are understood in varying ways, but a spiritual other world that may nevertheless be an intrinsic part of the everyday material world is a common theme.[22]

It was early on in my research that I came to the conclusion that I would have to include myself as an informant in my fieldwork to examine the depths of this mode of consciousness. This had the positive effect of breaking down the divisions between researcher and informant and Western and non-Western orientations to magic and has also helped me in my quest of creating a bridge of understanding between the different experiences and research languages of magic and academia. A reviewer of my first book, *Magic, Witchcraft and the Otherworld*, writing for the *American Ethnologist*, wrote that I gave a 'native's account', and that this contributed a 'unique twist' to experiential ethnography.[23] My experience of magical consciousness makes me a native, but we are all natives of this type of thought—in varying degrees. The difficulty is that anthropology is a discipline with theoretical and methodological understandings located firmly in the material world, despite attempts to value all human orientations as valid. Informants' relationships with spirits remain problematic to analysis, even more so because the anthropologist's experience of a spirit world as a fieldworker is expected to be involved, without 'going native', that is acquiesce to this reality.

Due to the problem of anthropological theories being bound within rationalistic discourses, it has been difficult finding explanatory frameworks that do not reduce the experience of magic to external terms or explanations that obliterate its essence. Many theories have implicit assumptions about the ultimate irrationality of magic or of the inferiority of magic when compared to science, or they reduce magic to its social or psychological effects, factors that can be understood more readily by the social sciences.

The exclusion of a sustained theoretical discussion of magic may reflect the overwhelming influence of sociological theories that 'exiled spirits to the margins of human experience, rendering them more the results of psychological aberrations than culturally understandable constructs'.[24] In this view, social relationships are primary and ritual, and belief systems are seen as reflections and expressions of society. A primary figure responsible for these theories is Emile Durkheim, the French sociologist mentioned previously. This position is also shown in the work of Henri Hubert (1872–1927) and Marcel Mauss (1872–1950), two members of *L'Année Sociologique* (the first sociology journal, of which Durkheim was an editor) who were concerned to show how magic was a social fact and not composed of mistaken and illogical processes of individual psychology. Hubert and Mauss thought that magic was a complex of ideas, beliefs and rites handed down from one generation to another.[25] Mauss defined magic by its social context and focussed on the symbolic meaning of magical acts. He contrasted magic with religion: in a religious rite, the individual was subordinated to social forces outside his or her power, but in magical rites, the individual appropriated the collective forces of society for his or her own ends.[26] The problems with these understandings, as we shall see in this book, are that they obscure vital dimensions of magical experience.

Things did not seem to bode well for my examination of the experience of magic, but as I re-read about an intellectual exchange on mystical mentality between philosopher Lucien Lévy-Bruhl (1857–1939), a contemporary and sympathizer of Durkheim, and anthropologist Edward Evans-Pritchard (1902–1973), I started to see the seeds of a new anthropology of magic. This exchange, that occurred almost a hundred years ago, seemed to provide the clues for a hidden thread of theoretical thought that would help a different understanding of magic. Lévy-Bruhl's work focused on the psychological aspects of collective native thought,[27] and it engaged Evans-Pritchard and had an influence on his subsequent writings. This classic debate made it clear that even though it was socially derived, mystical mentality was universal to all human beings: it was not just non-Western peoples who thought mystically as so-called civilized Westerners thought this way too, under certain conditions. Here was a theoretical thread that I could pursue in my own research, one that seemed to address important issues about the experience of magic.

Unfortunately, the important insights for the anthropology of magic opened up during the dialogue between Lévy-Bruhl and Evans-Pritchard are not well known in anthropology today. Early on, academics took a strong editorial line that preserved the growing dependence on the rationality of anthropology as a discipline. This grew into something of a myth (as an explanatory story), both in the grandness of the scenario and the lack of attention to the facts of the debate between the two men. This myth claims that the anthropologist Evans-Pritchard set the philosopher Lévy-Bruhl right on his erroneous views. Lévy-Bruhl had written extensively on native thought and had developed a notion of a pre-logical mind characterized as being a particular disposition that sees the world as filled with powers and entities not usually accessible to normal human senses—what we today would call a spirit world. For Lévy-Bruhl, prelogical thought was magicoreligious thought.[28] Anthropologists and others took the term *pre-logical* to be a racist assertion, and most, perhaps deliberately, chose not to try to understand what the philosopher was attempting to articulate, which was that due to different social conditions, native peoples tended to think mystically, rather than logically. A relatively recent example (in 2001) holds that Evans-Pritchard had an 'implicit argument' with Lévy-Bruhl, who 'adamantly argued that Africans were mired in a mystical "pre-logical" mentality'. It was apparently left to Evans-Pritchard to point out to Lévy-Bruhl that Azande thinking was no less rational than European thinking.[29] A case has been made here by these anthropologists against Lévy-Bruhl, accusing him of equating the term pre-logical with some form of inferior thinking, or even a prior evolutionary stage. This is not what Lévy-Bruhl had in mind at all.

Fortunately, Evans-Pritchard was not one of those anthropologists who ostracized Lévy-Bruhl, and he communicated with him to their mutual benefit, and for the benefit of anthropology, in furthering an understanding of human mentalities. The myth had it that Lévy-Bruhl recanted from his wrong thinking, but far from recanting, Lévy-Bruhl, while agreeing that the term pre-logical was confusing, spent the last part of his life clarifying and developing his concepts of mystical mentality. This was a continuation of his exploration of the human mind, a line of questioning that he had spent a lifetime studying and from which he never retrenched.[30]

The myth that Lévy-Bruhl was made to see the falsity of his thinking has obscured the importance of his work on magical modes of thought. It is unfortunate that Lévy-Bruhl's and Evans-Pritchard's early attempts to understand magic have resulted not in more development of their ideas, but rather a diversion of research into the effects of magic. This has concentrated attention on social issues, especially to do with maleficium and moral judgements concerning it, as to whether magic is good or evil, so-called white or black, and patterns of witchcraft accusations. The study of witchcraft, for example, has a long history within the discipline and has been examined as a set of beliefs, as rituals of verification, patterns of accusations and a social-strain gauge. Another line of enquiry was also to sidestep the question of the experience of magic altogether, and this was a focus on instrumentality—the art of influencing events or controlling spirits—funnelling analyses of magic into a rationality debate. This approach, while interesting in itself, had the effect of sidetracking ideas about the specific processes of human thought and put an emphasis on whether magic was true or false, and whether it could it be proved to exist. Lévy-Bruhl and Evans-Pritchard's dialogue on mystical mentality has suffered from neglect, and it is my aim in this work to explore further some of the issues that it raises concerning magic as a process of mind that goes beyond either sociological or psychological reduction.

The book is organized into four sections. The first section, 'Explaining Magic', seeks to do just that. It is composed of theories and ideas that I have found to be useful in trying to understand the experience of magic. Chapter 1 introduces the Lévy-Bruhl–Evans-Pritchard debate on mystical mentality, and Chapter 2 examines, through various examples, the important feature of mystical mentality expressed in Lévy-Bruhl's notion of participation, 'an orientation to the world based on an emotional association between persons and things in contact with a non-ordinary spirit reality'.[31] This chapter is an exploration of just some of the myriad ways that participation forms a psychic and sensory connection with material and nonmaterial reality. Participation characterizes a different orientation to the orientation of causality, the present scientific explanatory mode. I explore two more important theories for an understanding of the experience of magic in Chapter 3. The first is the notion of *sympathetic magic*, a term first coined by early-twentieth-century anthropologist James Frazer (1854–1941). While Frazer is ultimately dismissive of magic in comparison with science, his employment of sympathetic magic is helpful in understanding how magical ideas are formed through associations. The second notion is found in what has been termed *analogical thinking*. More recently, towards the end of the twentieth century, Stanley Jeyaraja Tambiah (1929–) pointed out the importance of magical thinking in the manner in which connections are made between one thing and another through the use of charms and spells; these connections are based on the *idea* that the one thing is like the other and the uniting point between them is magical. These chapters point out that the essence of an understanding of the experience of magic is not to be found in abstraction or any notion of causality, but rather, through a sense of association and connectedness.

In the next section, 'The Experience of Magic', comprising Chapters 4 and 5, I have tried to get close to what I consider to be the essence of magical consciousness by using my fieldwork. In these two chapters, I have used my own experience to delve deeper into the emotional aspects of participation. The first chapter in this section (Chapter 4) illustrates how emotion created an early connection with my grandfather that I had forgotten about, but which became apparent while working magically with a shaman. Chapter 5 shows the importance of the mythological imagination in shaping magical experience and providing a language for participation. Through a magical challenge, issued by witches whilst I was conducting fieldwork in East Anglia, England, I came to realize the importance of James Frazer's ideas about mythological associative thinking. In this case, the myth of the Wild Hunt, a European myth about a wild, nocturnal ride associated with the souls of the dead, provided a mythological context for a magical challenge of walking alone through a wood at night to encounter these spectral beings. This chapter also demonstrates participation through my enactment of a mythodrama based on the *Völuspá*, an Icelandic poem probably written in the late tenth century and recorded in the thirteenth-century *Prose Edda* by Snorri Sturluson (1179–1241), an Icelandic chieftain, poet and historian.

Chapters 6 and 7 form a section titled 'Practical Magic'. The first chapter in this section (Chapter 6) outlines Evans-Pritchard's landmark study of Azande witchcraft and magic practised as part of a system of beliefs intrinsic to society. Evans-Pritchard's *Witchcraft, Magic and Oracles among the Azande* (1937) opened up new horizons of understanding embedded in magical practices. Azande magic was not a passive object for the demonstration of an alien knowledge, but rather, a theory for understanding the nature of human experience. Evans-Pritchard showed that magic was a rational way of ordering society, but he did this at the expense of a complete analysis of mystical mentality. Chapter 7, while recognizing the value of Evans-Pritchard's work and the context in which he wrote it, seeks to redress the balance: magic is rational *and* mystical. It looks specifically at magic in everyday life through a focus on divination and healing. The latter includes a spirit component not normally accounted for in Western biomedical models, and the chapter gives various examples.

The last two chapters form a section titled 'Working with Magic'. In Chapter 8, I focus on the thorny issue of the reality of spirits—are spirits just imagination, or are they a human projection onto another realm? Another perspective of a holistic view of consciousness is put forward that helps locate magical consciousness as an experience of mind separate, but ultimately connected to, abstract analytical thinking. The final chapter tackles the challenging topic of re-visioning science so that magic can be considered as a legitimate form of knowledge. A metaphor of a web is used to envision this alternative attitude that can make magic visible and thus open to both understanding and critical evaluation, something that has been conspicuously absent in anthropology thus far.

This book tells a story about my journey to discover the anthropology of magic; it feels like a patchwork quilt or a jigsaw of pieces of information that I have picked up over the years, both in trying to make sense of my fieldwork experience and also in teaching ideas about magic in anthropology of religion courses at Goldsmiths College, University of London, and shamanic and altered states of consciousness courses at the University of Sussex. This journey could not have been undertaken, let alone written about, without the early encouragement and assistance of the late Olivia Harris and Pat Caplan, my teachers at Goldsmiths, and I would like to express my enormous gratitude to them for their support. Any errors or misinterpretations of the material are my responsibility alone.

I am also extremely grateful to Brian Bates, my magical partner and psychologist colleague at the University of Sussex, who has encouraged this project every step of the way; it is rare indeed to encounter someone who understands so intimately both the scientific and magical aspects of a work such as this, and I am deeply appreciative of his assistance. My sincere thanks also go to Jo Crow for friendship, her sharing of life history with me and for so many magical experiences.

Lise Paulsen Galal and Maruska Mosegaard invited me to give a keynote lecture on magical consciousness at the Danish Ethnographic Society and the Anthropologist Society in Denmark's 2007 annual meeting, and I was also invited by Kirsten Marie Raahauge to lead a 'Limits of Reason' Anthropological Research Group seminar at Copenhagen University in November 2007. Both these occasions helped me to develop my ideas about the analytical relevance of the concept of magic and to further understand how building on a newer theory of consciousness could throw light on a different explanation of magical experience; I thank all those involved. Øyvind Eikrem invited me to present a paper on magical healing given to the Rituals of Healing Conference, hosted by the Faculty of Health Sciences at Nord-Trøndelag University College, Norway, in 2008, and this brought another opportunity for exploration of these themes. I would like to thank him, and also Hanne Muller and Stein Johansen, for stimulating discussions.

I would also like to warmly thank Geoffrey Samuel and Barbara Tedlock for undertaking to review the manuscript of this book and for their endorsement. I am indebted to Hannah Shakespeare from Berg Publishers, for proposing the work in the first place and enthusiastically seeing it through the first stages of its preparation, and to Anna Wright, for coordinating the review stage before production.

Thanks are due to my daughter Lauren, who patiently checked the manuscript with an anthropological eye and to Brian Bates who checked it with a psychological eye, and to my long-term friend Annie Keeley, who also checked it for clarity and who has shared a good deal of the journey into magic with me. Finally, I would like to thank Adrian and Priscilla, and Roger Greenwood, for their continued support and encouragement.

## NOTES

1. See Henrietta Moore and Todd Sanders, eds, introduction to *Magical Interpretations, Material Realities: Modernity, Witchcraft and the Occult in Postcolonial Africa* (London: Routledge, 2001), for a discussion of the problems with using this term.
2. Adeline Masquelier, 'The Return of Magic', *Social Anthropology*, 12 (2004), pp. 95–102.
3. Peter Pels, introduction to Birgit Meyer and Peter Pels, eds, *Magic and Modernity: Interfaces of Revelation and Concealment* (Stanford: Stanford University Press, 2003), pp. 1–3.
4. Francis Yates, *Giordano Bruno and the Hermetic Tradition* (Chicago: University of Chicago Press, 1991).
5. Wikipedia List of Best-Selling Books, http://en.wikipedia.org/wiki/List_of_best-selling_books, accessed 14 July 2009.
6. See Pat Caplan, 'Terror, Witchcraft and Risk', *The AnthroGlobe Journal* [online journal] (19 Jan. 2001), http://www.anthroglobe.info/docs/caplanp_witchcraft_060119.htm, accessed 14 July 2009; Peter Geschiere, *On Witch Doctors and Spin Doctors: The Role of 'Experts' in African and American Politics* (Stanford: Stanford University Press, 2003).
7. Masquelier, 'Return of Magic'.
8. Caplan, 'Terror, Witchcraft and Risk'.
9. See, in particular, Meyer and Pels, *Magic and Modernity*, and Moore and Sanders, *Magical Interpretations*.

10. Roy Willis in Alan Barnard and Jonathan Spencer, eds, *Encyclopedia of Social and Cultural Anthropology* (London: Routledge, 2003), pp. 340–1.

11. Moore and Sanders, *Magical Interpretations*, p. 1.

12. This quote is from Valerie J. Flint, *The Rise of Magic in Early Medieval Europe* (Oxford: Clarendon Press, 1991), p. 15, and it records the views of the natural philosopher Pliny the Elder (AD 23–79) and Apuleius (*c.* AD 123–180), author of the bawdy Latin novel *The Golden Ass*.

13. Ariel Glucklich, *The End of Magic* (New York: Oxford University Press, 1997), p. 7.

14. *The Concise Oxford Dictionary of Current English*, 5th ed. (Oxford: Clarendon Press, 1964).

15. Thanks to Gordon MacLellan for bringing this article to my attention.

16. Richard Mabey, 'A Brush with Nature', *Wildlife* (March 2007), p. 13.

17. See Susan Greenwood, *The Nature of Magic* (Oxford: Berg, 2005), pp. 103–5.

18. In scientific experiments, it was important to exclude variables other than the one being tested; the experiment also had to be endlessly repeatable so that the results could be checked and the effects demonstrated. John Henry, *The Scientific Revolution and the Origins of Modern Science* (Basingstoke: Macmillan, 1997), p. 37.

19. Henry, *Scientific Revolution*, p. 37.

20. Henry, *Scientific Revolution*, p. 42.

21. Nigel Rapport and Joanna Overing, *Social and Cultural Anthropology: The Key Concepts* (London: Routledge, 2000), p. 274.

22. See, in particular, Susan Greenwood, *Magic, Witchcraft and the Otherworld* (Oxford: Berg, 2000).

23. Patric V. Giesler, 'Book Review: *Magic, Witchcraft and the Otherworld: An Anthropology*', *American Ethnologist*, 29 (2002), p. 208.

24. Jeannette Marie Mageo and Alan Howard, eds, *Spirits in Culture, History, and Mind* (New York: Routledge, 1996), pp. 2–3.

25. H. Hubert and M. Mauss, 'Esquisse d'une théorie générale de la magie', *L'Année Sociologique*, 7 (1902–3), quoted in E. E. Evans-Pritchard, 'Sorcery and Native Opinion', *Africa*, 4 (1931), pp. 23–8; excerpt reprinted in Max Marwick, ed., *Witchcraft and Sorcery* (London: Penguin, 1990), pp. 23–4.

26. Marcel Mauss, *A General Theory of Magic*, Robert Brain, trans. (New York: W. W. Norton, 1972).

27. For a critique of Lévy-Bruhl's psychological approach, see Mary Douglas, *Purity and Danger* (Harmondsworth: Penguin, 1970), pp. 92–4.

28. Evans-Pritchard, *Theories of Primitive Religion* (Oxford: Clarendon Press, 1990), p. 81.

29. Moore and Sanders, *Magical Interpretations*, p. 6.

30. Benson Saler, 'Lévy-Bruhl, Participation, and Rationality', in Jeppe Sinding Jensen and Luther H. Martin, eds, *Rationality and the Study of Religion* (London: Routledge, 2003), pp. 45–8.

31. Stanley Tambiah, *Magic, Science, Religion, and the Scope of Rationality* (Cambridge: Cambridge University Press, 1991), p. 91.

# SECTION ONE
# EXPLAINING MAGIC

This section sets out to explain theories that help an understanding of magic: not the explanations that somehow reduce magic to its effects on human behaviour or society, but the essence of magic as an intuitive process of mind. Magic is a holistic orientation to the world that is essentially relational and expansive; it is not irrational or confined to the thought of so-called primitives, nor is magic the preserve of non-Western, exotic societies. Rather, it is an aspect of human consciousness, and therefore it is especially appropriate to study magic in modern, Western societies, where it often manifests as an undercurrent.

# 1 MYSTICAL MENTALITY

Picture the scene of English anthropologist Edward Evans-Pritchard and French philosopher Lucien Lévy-Bruhl sitting opposite each other discussing mystical mentality in 1934. At such a meeting, what would they be conversing about, and why does it have such an implication for the study of magic? Evans-Pritchard and Lévy-Bruhl were formative in the early development of ideas about magic, and at the heart of this debate is an exploration of the very nature of human thought. Their exchange of ideas has huge implications for understanding magic in its essence as a human process of mind, and in this chapter, I have set out an imagined, constructed dialogue—a fictional documentary—built up from my reading of their correspondence and other related works. All of their conversation is based closely on their published ideas and, in some cases, actual correspondence. The bringing together of the universal grand schemes of thinking of the philosopher and the particular experience of the anthropologist reveals some interesting insights into the dynamics of an anthropological study of magic.

Returning to the ideas of these two early ancestor-type figures has established the parameters for a reconsideration of magic. In reading again their exchange of ideas for this book, I was struck by how their published work seemed so distant in time and obscured by debates over Lévy-Bruhl's use of the term pre-logical to describe native thought. In focusing on what I consider to be the real issues regarding magic and bringing them back into the present, I wanted to make it feel more immediate, closer to the experience of anthropologists in developing new ideas and new research methodologies. Some of the best work is done in dialogue with colleagues and in informal discussion at conferences and other gatherings. Seeking to capture this vitality, I visualized Evans-Pritchard and Lévy-Bruhl discussing mystical mentality as I researched their publications, respective biographical details and professional life histories; we know that they met personally, but we have no record of what was actually said.

Lévy-Bruhl had started a productive and stimulating exchange of ideas with Evans-Pritchard, who, in the early 1930s, wrote papers in Cairo in response[1]—one of which was published as 'Lévy-Bruhl's Theory of Primitive Mentality'—and he sent a copy to Lévy-Bruhl, whom he had met some time before. Evans-Pritchard had published the philosopher's reply to his paper, and in an introduction to Lévy-Bruhl's response, he wrote that it had value for students of the philosopher's writings; he also thought that the older man's 'tolerant, open-minded, and courteous' attitude was a 'model for any senior scholar replying to criticisms of his views by an inferior in years, knowledge, and ability'.[2] At this point, the philosopher would have been seventy-seven years old, while the anthropologist was thirty-two, less than half the older man's age. The action on the part of Evans-Pritchard indicates the high esteem in which he held Lévy-Bruhl, and it gives us a clue as to the basis of their relationship.

Before we venture into the imaginary dialogue, a few biographical details will give us greater insight into what the ramifications of the conversation might have been. Born in Crowborough, south-east England, in 1902, Evans-Pritchard studied history and anthropology at Oxford before going on to the London School of Economics (LSE), his intellectual base during his field trips to Africa. Charles Gabriel Seligman (1873–1940), a professor of ethnology at LSE,[3] had organized surveys of African cultures—tracing the territorial spread of people, mapping boundaries of language, culture and political domains—and he employed Evans-Pritchard as his research assistant. Some time later, Evans-Pritchard started his first fieldwork with the Azande, and it was during this period that he came to think that the anthropologist must live as far as possible in native people's villages and camps and to be physically and morally part of their community.

Evans-Pritchard was one of the first anthropologists to conduct such fieldwork and therefore to have first-hand information about how natives think. Before the turn of the century, the main sources of information for scholars were the detailed accounts of missionaries; those who studied these materials corresponded with the travellers, merchants, administrators and missionaries and interpreted their reports according to current theories—no one thought of doing systematic fieldwork. The two processes of collecting facts and theorizing were thought to be as different as spinning and weaving. Eventually, library analysis gave way to anthropology becoming professionalized.[4]

Unlike Evans-Pritchard, Lévy-Bruhl was dependent on the reports of others on native thought but was open to criticism and discussion from colleagues and ready to refine and develop his thinking. Born in Paris in 1857, Lévy-Bruhl was a contemporary of Durkheim, one of the founders of sociology, and his thinking is framed within Durkheimian social parameters. Lévy-Bruhl founded the Sorbonne Institute of Ethnology, Paris, but resigned in 1927 to spend time on writing and travel. A philosopher who was particularly fascinated with how people thought, Lévy-Bruhl wrote a number of books on the subject, ranging from *How Natives Think*, which was published in 1910, to *L'Expérience mystique et les symbols chez primitives*, published in 1937.

We can now turn to the conversation between the anthropologist and the philosopher on mystical mentality. We know from photographs that Lévy-Bruhl had a neatly trimmed moustache and a small, pointed beard; he wore small, round glasses, and his expression was often serious, even severe. In photographs, Evans-Pritchard looked the image of an elite English gentleman, and this belied his bohemian and nonconformist tendencies. Perhaps they are meeting in the faculty lounge at LSE or in a similar, book-lined room at Oxford University. They may be drinking a glass of wine, or perhaps a French brandy brought as a gift by Lévy-Bruhl.

## AN IMAGINARY DIALOGUE

*[As the two men settle into their seats, as the elder scholar at the end of his career, perhaps Lévy-Bruhl has a look that is both assured and searching, his head slightly inclined in listening position, as the anthropologist starts speaking. The younger anthropologist, who is in his prime, is just back from a trip to the homeland of the Azande in central Africa (the zone between the Nile and the Congo) and is fresh with ideas about magic. Evans-Pritchard is a practical man who was trained in history and uses plain common sense in his approach to ideas about magic. He is suspicious of the grand theoretical schemes of philosophers; nevertheless, he admires Lévy-Bruhl's work and considers him to be a great man and a great scholar. The first topic of conversation is some misunderstandings regarding the terminology that Lévy-Bruhl has used.[5]*

*Spending a lifetime researching the different ways in which humans think, Lévy-Bruhl was respectful of native thought. He had come to the view that native thinking processes were different to those of people in the West, —their thinking was mystical and pre-logical, rather than scientific. Influenced by the social orientation of Durkheim, he made a distinction between what he considered to be 'primitive' and 'civilized' societies. Today we obviously do not use the terms 'primitive' or 'civilized' in this manner, but at the time of this debate these terms were in common use (see Chapter 6, page 98).]*

### Evans-Pritchard:

Dear friend, I admire and have been greatly influenced by your work and I am concerned to break down misunderstandings about primitive mentality and what you have termed natives' prelogical thought because, as you know only too well, this has caused hostility amongst many anthropologists. We are agreed that the human mind thinks in similar ways, the problem is the language you use. Pre-logical is not a helpful term.

### Lévy-Bruhl:

I do not know how to thank you enough for the trouble which you have taken in order to arrive at the exact significance of my work, and to make it understood by the anthropologists who seem so hostile to it. If anything is capable of effectively combating the prejudice against me that exists in England, it is the exposition and examination of my theory to which you have devoted yourself in your writing.

*[Lévy-Bruhl had the habit of keeping a thin, inexpensive, black oilcloth notebook with thirty small pages of cross-ruled paper in his pocket, and if an idea in connection with his thoughts came to him, he would sit and write it down. These notebooks, which were first published posthumously as* Les Carnets de Lucien Lévy-Bruhl *in Paris in 1949 ten years after his death, related to the last months of his life, and the place and date where he had each thought appear underneath the wording of the text. Reading the notebooks, it is possible to follow Lévy-Bruhl on his outings in the Bois de Boulogne, at Bagatelle, and on the coasts of Normandy and Brittany and enter into some of his last thoughts on the human mind.[6] Perhaps he pulls one of these notebooks from his pocket now, as he consults his notes on how he would explain his views in English to Evans-Pritchard.]*

I do not think that primitives are incapable of thinking coherently, but I do believe that most of their beliefs are incompatible with a scientific view of the universe. These minds do not have, in some given circumstances, the same logical requirements as ours; they are logical, but the principles of their logic are different. There is a unity in the human mind in place and time, and primitive thinking is not due to an earlier evolutionary stage or inferior reasoning, but it is subject to different social conditions.

I decided to make a study of this mind in a society furthest from my own. I thought that the differences from Western mental habits were so great that no existing vocabulary could express them, and so I set out to create an adequate language. However, a closer examination has led me to move from seeing things from a logical point of view and abandon a badly founded hypothesis. I agree that the term prelogical suggests that native thinking is illogical, and this is not what I wanted to suggest at all.

## Evans-Pritchard:

*[The anthropologist smoked a pipe, and perhaps he relights it at this moment, as he considers what the philosopher has said.]*

I can see that you have tried to create a language to understand mystical mentality, and how you have sought to explain how primitive reasoning is incompatible with a scientific view of the world. In other words, native thought is mainly unscientific and also mystical. You refer to the content or patterns of thought that are social—social facts—not the processes of thinking that are psychological facts. So these thought processes are not based on a lack of mental ability but are due to different social conditions. Can you say more about this?

## Lévy-Bruhl:

Yes. What I am saying is that there are no biological or psychological differences between the thought of primitive and civilized people, but there are social differences. Natives' perceptions are different due to different social perceptions. Attention given to phenomena depends upon affective choice, and this is selective. Interest is controlled to a very large extent by the values given to phenomena by society—these values are expressed in collective representations, patterns of thought and behaviour.

Primitives think mystically, not scientifically, and they believe in forces, influences and actions that are imperceptible to the senses but are nonetheless real to them. There are two main types of society, each with a type of thought corresponding to it: civilized society is logically orientated; the causes of phenomena are located in natural, rather than mystical, processes, and thought is more individual. Primitive society, on the other hand, is oriented to the mystical; objects and beings are involved in a network of mystical participations, and here the focus is on collective representations, rather than individual thought. Collective representations give value to phenomena and direct peoples' attention, and it is society that shapes mystical mentality.

## Evans-Pritchard:

*[Evans-Pritchard was well known for his courtesy and for listening intently when in discussion with colleagues. He perhaps speaks in a diplomatic tone, although the gist of his comments are strong.]*

I think you have made too strong a contrast between primitive and civilized societies. I do not think you are really comparing what natives think with what Europeans think, but rather, the systematized ideology of native cultures with the content of individual minds in Europe. This is an abstraction based on collection of information about mystical beliefs held by a community about some phenomenon and pieced together into a coordinated ideological structure. The resulting pattern of belief may be a fiction since it may never be actually present in a person's consciousness at any time, and it may not be known in its entirety.

We need to compare like with like. Common sense should be compared with common sense, ritual with ritual, theology with theology, and so on. Scientific thought is a very specialized experience that only takes place in very specialized conditions; those who engage in it do not engage with it all the time: when out of the laboratory, they think like everyone else.

We do not conduct our lives as if we were conducting scientific experiment, nor do we think about religion like theologians. We are as prelogical as primitives in beliefs in religion, politics, morals, loyalties, families, countries and so on. We are shaped by collective representations, too—the flag, school, networks of sentiments, aspirations to an ideal; it is sentiment, not science, which sets the standard for living;

all sciences (the natural and the social) are a mixture of sentiment and experiment in their beginnings, and have only become separate over the centuries.

### Lévy-Bruhl:

Well, I agree. Primitive mentality oscillates between common sense and mystical thinking—it is both conceptual and affective. I use the term *mystical* for want of a better word; I do not mean it in a religious mysticism sense, but to describe a belief in forces, influences and actions that cannot be felt by the senses but are nevertheless real. Mystical mentality is more marked and more easily observable among primitive peoples, but it is present in every human mind. There is, I think, a permanent fund of mystical mentality that represents something fundamental and indestructible in the nature of human beings that enables poetry, art, metaphysics and scientific invention—almost everything, in short, that makes for the beauty and grandeur of human life.

However, what interests me is how primitive mentality is different from ours. In this respect, one problem is to find out how primitive people have such indifference to the most obvious and flagrant incompatibilities—they seem to have a lack of curiosity about the question of knowing how improbably, absurd and, according to us, impossible events occur. But what seems so natural to us does not occur to them. Participation, which is the basis of mystical mentality, is an attitude of mind that tolerates contradictions. If we can understand this, then we will see how the human mind has, little by little, adopted another attitude to life.

I do not deny that mystical elements exist in the mentality of English and French peoples, for example, but I think I ought to insist on the rational character of this mentality in order that differences from native thought might emerge clearly. I admit that I have presented primitive thought as more mystical and civilized thought as more rational than they in fact are, but it was done on purpose. I have no objection to saying that the primitive is not so exclusively mystical, or that civilized thought is not so consistently rational, once this difference is recognized, but I must say that twenty-five years ago, when I first started studying this, nobody had pointed it out. I wanted to bring fully to light the mystical *aspect* of primitive mentality to contrast it with the rational *aspect* of our societies. I am perhaps wrong in insisting strongly on differences, but I thought that anthropologists had done enough to make similarities evident. On this point, I think those who will follow us will know how to keep the right balance.[7]

### Evans-Pritchard:

Let us hope that they will know how to keep the right balance. What do you see as the essence of mystical mentality?

## Lévy-Bruhl:

*[Here we come to the essence of Lévy-Bruhl's view of magic.]*

The essence of mystical mentality is participation, for one thing to *participate* in something else. This is how mystical mentality works—everything is connected through relationship. Mystical thought connects one thing with another in a pattern of ideas and behaviours, and participation is the key. There is no sense of separation. There are no individuals as such; people are never other than parts of groups to which they belong. So you see, we have the organ with the body, the son or brother with the family, the grape with the bunch and so on. The representation of the individual occurs only secondarily and never alone; all form part of a participatory totemic essence. Participation is in the invisible and timeless essence of the group. Things that are distinct and separate from each other nevertheless participate with one another, sometimes to the point that they form only one. When a native perceives a tree, a bird or a fish, there are clearly some common elements between their representation and ours. The object is recognized to distinguish between a considerable number of species, subspecies and varieties; classification into long things, round things and so on; using generic images rather than concepts which are abstract; but the question is also of psychic recognition, and a reflex is set in motion of psychic connection with a pattern of relationships.

*[We can imagine that they talked o n well into the night, reflecting on various experiences and enjoying a feeling of conviviality.]*

\*\*\*

This conversation between anthropologist and philosopher shows that magic is not the domain of the so-called primitive mind, but rather, is part and parcel of everyday human thought and experience. The mentality of the individual is derived from the collective representations of society; certain ways of thinking belong to certain types of social structures.[8] In the course of various communications with Lévy-Bruhl, Evans-Pritchard argued that Lévy-Bruhl had made too strong a contrast between primitive and civilized societies:

| **Primitive Societies** | **Civilized Societies** |
| --- | --- |
| Mystical processes | Natural processes |
| Participation | Science |
| Collective | Individualistic |

Thinking that it was misleading to contrast primitive and civilized societies, Evans-Pritchard argued that Westerners do not think scientifically all the time, nor are they just individualistic. Western societies are shaped by collective representations, too, such as flag, school and networks of relationships. Evans-Pritchard was keen to avoid what he thought could be caricatures of primitive and modern thought. He thought that like should be compared with like in each specific society, and that mystical and scientific thought were best compared as normative ideational systems in the same society.

These two systems of thought were not mutually exclusive, and a person could behave mystically and then switch in another context to a more practical, everyday frame of mind.[9] Lévy-Bruhl was essentially in agreement with this and said that he only wanted to emphasize different aspects of human thought. The Lévy-Bruhl–Evans-Pritchard dialogue shifts the anthropological focus from how natives think to how the human mind thinks in particular social circumstances. All human beings think in similar ways; it is important to compare like with like *within* any given society.

Lévy-Bruhl was interested in examining human nature, and his training was philosophical, not anthropological, which led to the misunderstanding and hostility among many anthropologists. Lévy-Bruhl himself summed up the problem as follows:

> What can explain to a certain extent the evident misunderstanding among many anthropologists of my theory is the difference between the points of view in which they and I place ourselves. They relate what I say to the particular point of view of their science (which has its tradition, its methods, its achieved results etc.). What has led me to write my books is not the desire to add, if I could, a stone to the edifice of this special science (anthropology, ethnology). I had the ambition to add something to the scientific knowledge of human nature, using the findings of ethnology for the purpose. My training was philosophical not anthropological.[10]

It seems that the hostility generated by Lévy-Bruhl's work is less about the differences between anthropological and philosophical approaches and more about the issues that magic presents to anthropology as a rationalizing, social scientific discipline. Mystical mentality can be understood through its social effects on behaviour, but it is more easily apprehended through the experience of magic, and this has traditionally presented problems regarding the reality of invisible forces, as we have already seen in the introduction and will come back to in Section 4, particularly Chapter 8.

The real value of Lévy-Bruhl's thinking on mystical mentality is his aim to study human nature through the adoption of a philosophical concept called *participation*, a defining characteristic of mystical mentality. Participation is the key to an understanding of magic, and we will explore what it means in the next chapter.

## NOTES

1. Stanley Tambiah, *Magic, Science, Religion, and the Scope of Rationality* (Cambridge: Cambridge University Press, 1991), p. 87.
2. Lévy-Bruhl, 'A Letter to E.E. Evans-Pritchard', *British Journal of Sociology*, 3 (1952), pp. 117–23.
3. 'Charles Gabriel Seligman', http://southernsudan.prm.ox.ac.uk/biography/seligman/, accessed 14 July 2009.
4. Mary Douglas, *Evans-Pritchard* (Brighton: Harvester, 1980), pp. 39–41.
5. For this imagined dialogue, I am indebted to the following: Maurice Leenhardt, preface to *The Notebooks on 'Primitive' Mentality*, Peter Riviere, trans. (Oxford: Basil Blackwell, 1975); Lévy-Bruhl, 'A Letter'; Jean Cozeneuve, *Lucien Lévy-Bruhl: sa vie, son œuvre* (Paris: Presses Universitaires de France, 1963); Douglas, *Evans-Pritchard*.
6. Leenhardt, preface to *Notebooks on 'Primitive' Mentality*.
7. This is a specific reference to what Lévy-Bruhl says in his letter to Evans-Pritchard; Leenhardt, preface to *Notebooks on 'Primitive' Mentality*.
8. See Evans-Pritchard, *Theories of Primitive Religion* (Oxford: Clarendon Press, 1990), p. 80, and Mary Douglas, *Purity and Danger* (Middlesex: Penguin, 1970), pp. 93–4.
9. Tambiah, *Magic, Science, Religion*, p. 92.
10. Lévy-Bruhl, 'A Letter', p. 123.

## FURTHER READING

Douglas, Mary, *Purity and Danger*, Middlesex: Penguin, 1970, pp. 92–4.

Evans-Pritchard, Edward, *Theories of Primitive Religion*, Oxford: Clarendon Press, 1990. Orig. publ. 1965.

Lévy-Bruhl, Lucien, 'A Letter to E.E. Evans-Pritchard', *British Journal of Sociology*, 3 (1952), pp. 117–23.

Lévy-Bruhl, Lucien, *The Notebooks on Primitive Mentality of Lucien Lévy-Bruhl*, Peter Riviere, trans., Oxford: Basil Blackwell, 1975.

Wiebe, Donald, 'Mythopoetic and Scientific Thought', in *The Irony of Theology and the Nature of Religious Thought*, Montreal: McGill-Queen's Press, 1991, pp. 46–79.

# 2 PARTICIPATION: A KEY TO UNDERSTANDING MAGIC

First and foremost a philosopher, it must have seemed natural to Lévy-Bruhl to adopt the philosophical concept of participation to try to make sense of mystical mentality. The concept works well to describe the associative experience that sums up a magical attitude of mind. Participation forms its own holistic language of connections that are both social and individual. A form of mental processing that happens through a shift in consciousness, this change in awareness makes associations and connections between things, situations and feelings. Lévy-Bruhl gave a number of examples to show how the concept worked to create a psychological link between things, including explaining how a shaman could be a human as well as any number of guardian spirits that she may have. Participation is a concept that describes this process, and it incorporates stages ranging from seemingly ordinary and mundane levels to a profound experience that radically changes a person's life, as in a shamanic initiation. Here in this, its more extreme form, participation is transformative in relation to the everyday material world. The shaman feels that her bodily boundaries dissolve to such an extent that feelings of personal connectedness and empathy are intense.

A contemporary example of a more everyday expression of participation comes from my experience while I was writing this book. Staying in a remote Welsh cottage overlooking the Preseli mountains in Pembrokeshire, I decided to note down my thoughts as a way of trying to explain the seemingly everyday experience:

> The clouds crossing the sun cast the mountainside into an enormous moving tapestry of dancing light ranging from pale yellows and mellow greens to darkest slate grey. The Preselis are said to be the entrance to Annwn, the Celtic underworld. As the light skitters over and caresses the land forming endless patterns, the remains of a small stone circle standing in front of me calls from a distant past. The call is echoed at Stonehenge, many miles to the south-east, where the inner circle of stones were taken from here by Neolithic people. A wren cocks her head up and down as she darts from branch to branch in an old, wizened ash tree. I look up into the clear blue sky, and a buzzard circles in the air overhead. I feel the past connected with the present in the precise moment.

Some time later, still in a participatory state of mind, I walk on Newport Beach, some four miles or so farther north:

> Later, the tide comes rushing up the sand like little lace frills on a dainty petticoat; momentarily it twirls into froth and then recedes back into the waves. The firm sand underfoot echoes the movement in small rivulets. The air is clear and fresh and I breathe deeply, aware of the precious moment in time. The bay sweeps before me in an arc and I notice that the rocks are dark slate-coloured stone. As I walk closer I see that the cliff opens out into a cave that looks like a great slit into the centre of the earth; a feminine entrance. Negotiating the rock pools at the entrance of the cave is like walking through a maze—the rock forms a pattern criss-crossed with small waterways filled with different coloured seaweeds; small fish dart between my toes.
>
> The darkness of the huge grey rock looms large and I make my way into the fissure. Deep in the cave I go back in time [in my imagination] to a cave I visited in Lascaux, in the Dordogne, France. The image before me is a 'falling horse', a Palaeolithic image painted on the cave wall between 15,000 and 10,000 BC. Was it here deep within caves that human beings first experienced magic? Did this upside down horse that is painted right into the crack in the rock take people into another world in an altered state of consciousness?

A number of points can be made about my example of participation:

1. Associated with altering levels of consciousness, participation is immediate and present in the moment. I am drawn into the dancing light on the mountains, the movement of birds, the presence of the stone circles—the small one before me and Stonehenge, the larger, famous one on Salisbury Plain, the site of Druid Summer Solstice rituals—and into the sea and the cave, which transports me, in my memory, to Lascaux. The connections made are intuitive, rather than analytically considered.

2. The language of participation is a language of holism that has a continuity of space and time—the past is connected with the present, and the Neolithic stone circles seem to be connected and a part of the moment; I can use participation to think about altered states of consciousness and magic in relation to the Lascaux Palaeolithic cave paintings I have seen in France.

3. Often expressed in a metaphorical mode that evokes the emotions and develops a psychic connection with other phenomena, the concept of participation helps me to express how I feel at one with the mountainside, the sea and the cave. Writing like this tends to be depicted via a poetic turn of phrase.

4. Participation can invoke an inspirited orientation to the world; the way that Lévy-Bruhl used the term can be likened to *animism*, a term first coined by early

English anthropologist Edward Burnett Tylor (1832–1917) to describe a world view that considered soul or psyche to be within all things, animate as well as what we would perhaps consider to be inanimate. For Aristotle (384–322 BC), an early Greek philosopher, soul was equivalent to psyche—'the principle of life' that animates a living creature; only more recently has psychology developed as a discipline to study psyche as something that refers solely to the human head.

5. According to Lévy-Bruhl, participation forms a mythical world. The reference that links the Preselis with the Celtic underworld indicates a common theme—that such places are entrances to a spiritual other world, a deeper aspect of consciousness, a place of knowledge and wisdom that can be accessed through the magical aspect of mind.

---

**Key Features of Participation**

Utilizes an altered state of consciousness

Employs a language of holism

Uses a metaphorical mode

Engages with an inspirited world view

Draws us in to a mythological realm expressed through stories

---

Opening a door into deeper resonances, participation is an orientation to the world that can be expressed through mythologies and stories. This was made very clear to me when I was first starting my research on magic, and the realization was made through a conversation with a witch who lived in a small house in Bradford, northern England. I had been given her name by the first person who I had interviewed, who was a friend of hers. This witch, whom I called Leah, was a large, powerful woman in her mid-thirties with long, dark hair, and she was a member of a coven that was connected with Reclaiming, a witchcraft community in San Francisco. Leah invited me to dinner, and during the meal, she explained that she was a storyteller, and she told me how her stories were spells that could change people's lives. All practitioners of magic know the importance of altering consciousness if they are to experience a magical mode of mind, and Leah was no exception. Leah knew this particularly well. She thought that her stories spoke to people's unconscious minds:

> If I choose the stories I can effect change without anybody knowing what
> I'm doing because stories are spells, they're changing on two levels, working

on the conscious and the unconscious. I don't have to say to people 'I'm working on your unconscious now', I don't have to say that. If I've done my work right something will happen and it does, it works. I will see the look or someone will go 'ah!'. My stories are almost all about transformation in some way, they are quite deep. That is the sort of work that I can do because I'm doing what I don't appear to be doing and that's how I deal politically with the Craft. I do what I don't appear to be doing. I have a lot of Scorpio [astrological birth sign] in me, secretive. I believe that myths work utterly.

Leah had a captivating presence, and I could feel myself being drawn into what she was saying. The art of storytelling is an ancient one, and we can imagine the people who used to inhabit caves, such as those at Lascaux, sitting around a fire in the evenings listening to tales of how the world came to be as well as everyday events and happenings. Stories and myths are a language of participation—they take us deep into our imagination, where different experiences are possible, and this is the transformation of consciousness that Leah talks about. We will explore this important aspect of magic further in Chapter 5, and we will also return to the important role of myths and stories later in this chapter, but for the present, we will delve a little deeper into Lévy-Bruhl's exposition of participation.

## LÉVY-BRUHL'S MAGICAL PARTICIPATION

Let us explore what Lévy-Bruhl has to say about participation through a number of key points, all of which involve notions of connectedness, namely, psychic connection, connection with a dream world, connection between humans and animals and connection between the living and the dead.

### Psychic Connection

*Question:* Why does a hunter strike a spear into the imprint of an animal?

*Answer:* Participation is based on what Lévy-Bruhl called *pars pro toto*—the notion that the part is equivalent to the whole. For example, a hunter might strike a spear into an imprint left by an animal. The aim is to wound the animal because to wound the footprint is the same as wounding the animal. A hunter who strikes a spear into a footprint left by an animal being tracked makes a psychic connection with it.

\*\*\*

*Question*: Why does a magician pierce a waxen image of his victim?

*Answer*: If a magician pierces a waxen image of a victim, the result is the piercing of the person at one and the same time because the present is in the future. This is in contrast to our detached view that sees a whole being composed of parts, the part being smaller than the whole. The native community of essence is an identity felt between what participates and what is participated in—for example there is a relationship between an individual and his appurtenances (hair, nails, excretions, clothing, footprints, shadow etc.), a symbol and what it represents, a corpse and a ghost, the living and the dead, mythical ancestors and totems and so on.

## Connection with a Dream World

*Question:* How can a person be in two places at once?

*Answer*: The dream world is as real as the waking world. For example, a missionary is accused of stealing a pumpkin from a garden. He explains that he cannot have committed the theft because he was 150 miles away. The native accuser acknowledges this but still persists with his claim. In a dream, the accuser saw the man enter the garden, take the pumpkins and leave with them. In the dream, the man did enter the garden, and the dream is believed as real. The accuser accepts that the man was 150 miles away, but he also believes that on the same day, he took the pumpkin. How can two simultaneous presences happen? asks the philosopher. The accuser is not a fool and reasons normally, and something felt as real is definitely real, whether possible or not. He argues that natives will put up with what are, to Westerners, two incompatible certainties and will not feel obliged to choose between them. In this case, the personality of the man participates in two places at once—in what are to us the material reality and the dream. Personality is not limited to the periphery of the physical body; personality can be in different places at the same time.

## Connection between Humans and Animals

*Question:* How can a person be an animal as well as human?

*Answer*: An account of a female shaman in Oregon shows how individuals are simultaneously humans and animals. Shamans customarily have a number of guardian spirits, and this shaman has five, who make their appearance successively in dreams: they come as a bear, yellow hammer, otter and so on. They also reveal themselves in human form and speak to her. One such guardian spirit is a bear, who appears as a man but says he is a spirit. He reveals what he is ready to do in order that the woman may become 'a big doctor', and he tells her the conditions that she must fulfil for this to occur. At another time, he appears as a bear, rather than a man. What appears as a man or as a bear is of no importance—he is both—and he shows himself sometimes as one and sometimes as the other.

***

*Question*: Why do witches transform into animals?

*Answer*. Witches use their power to change form to achieve certain ends. For example, witches transform into rats, which damage coconuts, or they send rats to do the damage; either the witch causes his victim to be seized by a real crocodile on his orders, or he is himself that crocodile. The question of which is which has no interest—the power and the action for the witch are alone what is important. In native eyes, the witch has the power to turn himself into a leopard, that is to say, one now sees him in human form; a few minutes ago, one saw him in the form of the leopard, and perhaps he is going to resume that form in a moment. This transformation takes place as soon as he enters the skin of the leopard and ceases as soon as he leaves it (for natives, a change of skin is equivalent to a change of body). In short, in successive moments, the witch is either man or else leopard. It is probable that, if he wished, he might be another animal or a plant or some other thing. Natives do not see any difficulty here: the myths teach that the form of individuals is only an accident. What matters is the *power to take* this or that form.

## Connection between the Living and the Dead

*Question:* How can a corpse become a ghost?

*Answer*. A deceased person can become a ghost because a deceased person is at one and the same time the ghost who wanders in the neighbourhood and the immobile corpse on the bed. Participation is a given—it does not come after representation of the corpse and the ghost by concepts. The corpse and the ghost represent a single unity—people participate in one another through feeling. It is a complex of affective elements and representative elements: emotion caused by the death, the felt participation; the isolated representation of either the corpse or the ghost, which, if it comes, comes only afterwards.[1] For Westerners, death causes a separation between the individual and the mortal remains—we picture the ghost and the corpse. So we think differently: we take two separate terms or things first, and only establish a feeling of participation afterwards. Natives do not make separate representations as explicit as we do: a soul (spirit, immaterial reality) is spiritual and material. Corpse and ghost are always felt as one individual. If we are to understand participation, we have to renounce our concepts of separateness of phenomena.

***

As Lévy-Bruhl has shown, participation is rich and varied: it ranges from the manner in which a hunter will track and pursue an animal to notions of death and ghosts. I have put together four other wide-ranging examples to give a feel for some different degrees of participation: from the relatively mundane way a place like London expresses personal identity to the mystical relationship with a saint in Morocco; a Native American clan legend; and finally, a myth told widely in Asia about a shamanic transformation into a bird to effect the healing of an emperor.

## Magical Habits of Mind

My first example of participation comes from the work of Jonathan Raban, a journalist, novelist and political commentator. In his book *Soft City*, he tells of his participation with place through what he calls 'magical habits of mind'. He finds the city of London a place of expression of his identity. Raban sees the city as a place for the expression of personal identity as soft, fluid and open to the will and to the imagination. The city is a theatre: a series of stages upon which individuals can 'work their own distinctive magic while performing a multiplicity of roles'. Cities, unlike villages and small towns, he argues, are plastic by nature. 'We mould them in our images: they, in turn, shape us by the resistance they offer when we try to impose our own personal form on them.'[2] Living in a city, a person slips unconsciously into 'magical habits of mind'. The city is mapped by private benchmarks that are meaningful only to that individual; a city is individually shaped with boundaries, transportation points and wildernesses: 'like any tribesman hedging himself in behind a stockade of taboos, I mark my boundaries with graveyards, terminal transportation points and wildernesses. Beyond them, nothing is to be trusted and anything might happen.'[3]

Inside London, Raban's private city, there is a grid of reference points of personal attribution of meaning: 'a black-fronted bookshop in South Kensington, a line of gothic balconies on the Cromwell Road'.[4] Symbols denote a particular quarter—the underground may, for example, turn into an object of superstition, an irrational way of imposing order on the city: 'the Piccadilly Line is full of fly-by-nights and stripe-shirted young men who run dubious agencies.'[5] Raban suggests that there is more than a merely vestigial magicality in the way people live in cities—magic is a way of surviving living in the city.

While Raban's language reflects a Western sense that magic is irrational, it does illustrate the language of participation—of living in the city with a magical frame of mind; it is possible to identify with various aspects of city life and create meaning-ful connections with place through conceptual maps—an 'improvised day-to-day magic'.[6] Magic may be a major alternative to rejection of the city as a bad, unmanage-able place, and 'it offers a real way of surviving in an environment whose rationale has, like a dead language, become so obscure that only a handful of specialists (alas, they are all too frequently sociologists, urban economists and town planners) can remember or understand it'. Raban claims that 'the rest of us make do with an im-provised day-to-day magic, which, like shamanism, works because we conspire that it shall work'.[7] This is the everyday type of magic that people use as they go about their everyday lives.

## Visiting the Saint

The experience of participation, as a feeling of connection, is probably similar in essence for most people, but it is explained in different ways in different contexts. In one culture, it might be mystical, and in another, magical or religious; but the underlying experience is likely to be comparable. Sometimes mystical experience can be located in special people or geographical areas, as in Morocco's cult of saints:

> Moroccans speak of visiting a saint's sanctuary as 'visiting *the* saint', for they believe him to be alive in his sanctuary . . . in certain instances—for example, when Tuhami, [the informant in question] talks about going to 'Moulay Id-riss'—there is even greater ambiguity, for 'Moulay Idriss' refers not only to the saint, and to his sanctuary but to the village in which his sanctuary is located, the village in which he resides.
>
> Associated with the saints is a gamut of rituals, ranging from the com-munal recitation of supernumerary prayers and highly stylized trance dances to special massages with rocks endowed with *baraka*, baths in waters sacred to the saint, the removal of a handful of earth from the saintly sanctuary, or simply the circumambulation of the saint's tomb. Pilgrims frequently sleep in the sanctuary in the hope of having a dream; such dreams are thought to be

messages from the saint or even visitations. Some Moroccans, like Tuhami, claim that the saints are alive in their tombs. For them the saints resemble rather more the *jnun* than deceased human beings. . .

The sanctuaries . . . are visited by pilgrims anxious for a cure for any ailment, ranging from a bout of rheumatism or menstrual cramps to demonic attack and spirit possession. They are visited, too, for poetic inspiration, acrobatic prowess, success in business or school, for the birth of a male child or the preservation of a marriage, or simply for those feelings of well-being that are associated with the gift of *baraka*. Most often, supplicant pilgrims promise to sacrifice something, a sheep, a goat, or perhaps a seven-colored chicken, or to give something, food, candles, or money to the saint, if he responds to their supplication. Such a pledge binds the supplicant to the saint, and failure to carry it out will result in great harm to him or his family: they will become vulnerable to the demons, for the saint will remove his protection if indeed he does not incite the *jnun* to attack.[8]

A personal participatory mystical relationship is forged with the saint. The mystical presence of the saint extends to the whole geographical location—the personal relationship is also with the specific village, the area endowed with magical power by association with the saint. Rituals, prayers and trance dances help to intensify this participatory bond in the pilgrim's consciousness, as does massage with rocks infused with spirit, baths taken in sacred waters and taking earth from the shrine. The saint is believed to have a special power, an instrumental magic—he can help with ailments, inspiration and business. A sacrifice binds a contract that is reinforced through the threat of spirit attack if the binding pledge is not carried out.

## Blessings from the Mussel

Writing about North American Indian vision quests, American anthropologist Ruth Benedict (1887–1948) shows how the Southern Plains Osage explain their clan totem by virtue of a vision quest whereby each clan ancestor sought a vision and was blessed by the animal whose name the clan inherited. This legend, as Benedict explains it, helps the members of the mussel clan to identify with their totem animal, so much so that their bodies are inextricably linked; they will live long lives and will not be subject to the power of the gods. As the legend goes, the ancestor of the mussel clan, with tears running down his face, sought this blessing from a mussel:

O grandfather,
The little ones have nothing of which to make their bodies.
Thereupon the mussel answered him:
You say the little ones make of me their bodies.

When the little ones make of me their bodies,
They shall always live to see old age.
Behold the wrinkles upon my skin [shell]
Which I have made to be the means of reaching old age.
When the little ones make of me their bodies
They shall always live to see the signs of old age upon their skins
The seven bends of the river [of life]
I pass successfully.
And in my travels the gods themselves have not the power to see the trail that
   I make.
When the little ones make of me their bodies
No one, not even the gods, shall be able to see the trail they make.[9]

The body of the mussel clan totem is the body of the ancestor and is the body of individuals in the clan, and all participate in blessings. The concept of participation creates a link between individual, clan and the mussel ancestor; these are not discrete entities, but rather, are part and parcel of a whole pattern of understandings and related behaviour.

## Healing the Emperor

In the next example, there is a similar participatory connection, this time between a shaman and his spirit helper. The specialist consciousness of a Daur shaman may be extended into other beings in a manner commonly described as shape-shifting. In its more extreme forms, participation involves such a depth of emotional empathy that everyday physical bodily boundaries are dissolved, as in the following story:

> The Emperor in the capital city fell ill, but none of his Buddhist lamas' remedies worked, try as they might. The Emperor called a famous Daur shaman to cure him. Now around the empire there was the Great Wall and the Daurs were outside it. How could the shaman get through the wall? His ordinary human body could go, but an Imperial edict forbade the entry of shamans' spirits, even though on this occasion the Emperor himself needed them. The shaman journeyed for many days and arrived at the great gate of the wall. He stopped and concentrated all his spirits [*onggor*] and transformed them into a small bird. At this moment a carter was trundling through and in his right hand he was holding up a long whip with a leather tip. The bird perched joyfully on the top of this whip and rode though the gate. It flew straight to Beijing and into the palace. There was a hell of a fight and the Emperor was cured.[10]

The consciousness of the shaman participates with the bird to heal the Emperor. This participation between a shaman and a bird involves contradictions to the dominant, Western manner of thinking; this participatory mode has an implicit indifference to what seems like flagrant contradictions to causal, analytical logic. Participation is an attitude of mind that tolerates logical contradictions that a person can be a human being and a bird simultaneously. If, as Lévy-Bruhl suggested, we are to understand participation, we have to renounce our concepts of separateness of phenomena and entertain the possibilities of flexible, transient and transformatory boundaries between things.

## ALTERNATIVE VIEWS OF PARTICIPATION

Earlier in this chapter, we saw how stories and myths are important to the process of changing consciousness to a participatory mode of mind; however, it would be a mistake to think that stories and myths are only the province of magical participation. Plato, an early Greek philosopher (427 BC–AD 347), knew the importance of myth and told a story about a cave, but with a very different message about participation. As we have already seen, Lévy-Bruhl was a philosopher, and he used the philosophical concept of participation to describe mystical mentality; Plato, on the other hand, told stories about the intellect rather than the senses.

Plato's view of participation describes a world that had to be expressible in mathematical terms, mathematics being the most precise and definite kind of thinking and important for scientific thought. Pythagoras, another early Greek philosopher (born between 580 and 572 BC and died between 500 and 490 BC), had shifted the focus of attention from the matter of the everyday world to forms or ideas. Pythagoras gave mathematics a mystical significance by viewing the nature of things in numbers—this suggested an inherent order of the universe. Pythagoras thought that the essence of being was in number, and this influenced Plato and initiated the rationalist tradition in philosophy, whereby an eternal world was revealed to the intellect, not the senses. Plato considered mathematical objects as perfect forms, for example he describes a line as an object having length but no breadth. No matter how thin we make a line in the world of the senses, it will not be like the perfect mathematical form; it will always have breadth. Objects in the real world tried to be like their perfect forms but they never succeeded,[11] and it is here that Plato uses a myth to illustrate the unreliability of the senses:

> Imagine a cave deep in the earth. Inside the cave are some prisoners chained
> and sitting in near darkness. The only dim light comes from a fire near the
> entrance of the cave. Between the chained prisoners and the fire there is a low
> wall on which people carrying statues move. The prisoners, who cannot turn
> around to see what is behind them, see the shadows cast on the back wall of

the cave and they think these shadows are the whole of reality. When the prisoners emerged from the cave into the sunshine they realized that what they had taken for reality was just shadows.

For Plato, sense perceptions—as the experience of the shadows within the cave—are untrustworthy. We are imprisoned within our own bodies and minds, and we cannot find our real selves.[12] True knowledge can only be understood through the thought of Ideas formed from an eternal and unchanging world that exists unto itself. Plato made a dualism between the ordinary world of visible and tangible things (the cave) and a superior world of Ideas, a timeless and nonsensory reality.[13] In the *Middle Dialogues*, he employed the notion of participation to describe the relationship between the realm of Being, the superior, transcendent world of Ideas, and a realm of Becoming, an inferior and dependent world of experience.[14]

Here we can see that this platonic use of the term participation differs from Lévy-Bruhl's. Whereas Plato saw one distinct entity participating in another—a realm of Becoming that existed and had apparent qualities only because it participated in a realm of nonsensory Being—Lévy-Bruhl saw participation as a sensory and psychic connection with both material and nonmaterial reality. Lévy-Bruhl's conception of participation is not dualistic, but monistic. *Monism* is a term originating in the mid nineteenth century from the Greek *monos*, meaning 'single'; it is a viewpoint that denies the separateness of phenomena, or put another way, it is a view that makes no distinction between spirit and the material world. There is no reference to a superior transcendent realm; the mystical world is the everyday world, and spirit inhabits material reality. The differences between Plato and Lévy-Bruhl can be seen in the following table:

| **Plato's Participation** | **Lévy-Bruhl's Participation** |
|---|---|
| Reason | Emotion |
| Senses unreliable | Sensory and psychic connections |
| * | * |
| Inferior realm of Becoming participates in a superior realm of Being | An affective disposition that forms a mythical world not governed by laws or time |
| Dualistic | Monistic |

It is Plato's conception of participation that has had an impact on the manner in which social scientists and scholars of religious studies have viewed magic.[15] Romanian philosopher and historian of religion Mircea Eliade (1907–1986) takes up this platonic theme of participation in his examination of the differences between mythological and historical time. Eliade's platonic conception sees the material world as having extraterrestrial archetypes that work as an 'exemplary model' for what exists on a higher cosmic level. Through rituals and rites, profane time is suspended and humans are projected into the mythical epoch in which the archetypes were first revealed; the profane time of history is abolished, and something—an act or an object—only becomes real if it repeats or imitates an archetype. Mythological time was an ontology (concerned with the nature of being[16]) that he associated with archaic and traditional societies; a time when people felt themselves deeply connected with cosmic rhythms. Objects or acts acquired a value and became real because they participated in a reality that transcended them. Everyday artefacts created by people from nature 'acquire their reality, their identity, only to the extent of their participation in a transcendent reality'.[17]

Thus it can be seen that the concept of participation can be used in two ways, but it is the monistic, rather than the dualistic, interpretation that particularly interests us in our study of magic as a mode of thought.

## TWO COEXISTING ORIENTATIONS

Lévy-Bruhl answered criticisms from fieldworkers, such as Evans-Pritchard, and admitted that he had made so-called primitive peoples more mystical than they really were. It was the relationship between the two modes of thought that had interested Evans-Pritchard, who pointed out that it was not so much a question of so-called primitive versus civilized mentality as the relation of two types of thought to each other in any society. In Lévy-Bruhl's later work, *L'expérience mystique et les symboles* and *Carnets*, he considered that the thought of small-scale peoples oscillated between common sense and mystical orientations.[18]

Taking up the theme of different modes of consciousness in his book *Magic, Science, Religion, and the Scope of Rationality*, Stanley Jeyaraja Tambiah says that people everywhere have two coexisting orientations to the world. The first is causality, which emphasises atomistic individualism and distance, and the second is participation, an orientation to the world which places that person in the world fully as a totality and where action is often expressed through myth and ritual.[19] Participation is an emotional experience that does not rely on the logical, causal mode of thought, and it is personal to the individual's senses. As a mode of thought, participation exists alongside causality, a logical thinking that is abstract, separated and focused.

The differences between causal thinking and participatory thinking can be summed up as the distinction between scientific technical orientations and magico-religio-mythological orientations. While there are distinct differences between participatory thinking and causal thinking, it is a mistake to make a radical distinction between

*Causality*: Ego against the world; egocentricity. Atomistic individualism: The language of distancing and neutrality of action and reaction; the paradigm of evolution in space and time; instrumental action that changes matter and the causal efficacy of technical acts; the successive fragmentation of phenomena, and their atomization, in the construction of scientific knowledge.

*Participation*: Ego/person with the world, a product of the world; sociocentrism; the language of solidarity, unity, holism and continuity in space and time; expressive action that is manifest through conventional intersubjective understandings, the telling of myths and the enactment of rituals; the performative efficacy of communicative acts; pattern recognition and the totalization of phenomena; the sense of encompassing cosmic oneness.[20]

them. Participation and causality do not form a dualism, but rather, intertwine in any one person's mind; these aspects of thinking are not diametrically opposed; rather, they intertwine in the wider process of consciousness[21]:

> So, although 'causation' and 'participation' may seem different or contrastive orientations to the world, both are experienced and symbolized through the same human senses of touch, taste, hearing, seeing. Much of the discourse of causality and positive science is framed in terms of distancing, neutrality, experimentation, and the language of analytic reason, while much of the discourse of participation can be understood through sensory and emotional communication. Crucially, neither can exclude the other.[22]

Causal orientations occur within formal frameworks and participation usually happens during social ritual events, although these are ideal type constructions and the two modes of thought can potentially occur in a whole range of different scenarios. In actual practice, we all probably use both types of thinking intermittently.

In the next chapter, we will explore two other explanations for this holistic type of awareness, namely, sympathetic magic and analogical thinking.

## NOTES

1. Notebook (Jan.–May 1938), pp. 1–4.
2. Jonathan Raban, *Soft City* (London: Hamish Hamilton, 1974), p. 9.
3. Raban, *Soft City*, p. 166.
4. Raban, *Soft City*, p. 167.
5. Raban, *Soft City*, p. 168.
6. Susan Greenwood, *The Nature of Magic* (Oxford: Berg, 2005), pp. 210–11.

7. Raban, *Soft City*, p. 169.
8. This is taken from Vincent Crapanzano, *Tuhami, Portrait of a Moroccan* (Chicago: University of Chicago Press, 1980), pp. 16–17; quoted in Stanley Tambiah, *Magic, Science, Religion, and the Scope of Rationality* (Cambridge: Cambridge University Press, 1991), pp. 106–7.
9. Ruth Benedict, *Patterns of Culture* (New York: Mentor Books, 1948), pp. 36–7.
10. Caroline Humphrey with Urgunge Onon, *Shamans and Elders* (Oxford: Clarendon Press, 1996), p. 8.
11. 'Plato', http://www-history.mcs.st-and.ac.uk/Biographies/Plato.html, accessed 12 March 2009.
12. The existence of two realms is the same for humans—there is a part that can be seen and an underlying part that cannot be seen but of which our minds are capable of achieving awareness. Human bodies, as material objects, also inhabit this realm of space and time, subject to laws of physics; they exist, ever changing, and pass away. However, bodies offer a fleeting glimpse of something nonmaterial, timeless and indestructible—that is a soul. Souls are permanent forms that inhabit the timeless, spaceless existence that is unchanging—this is ultimate reality. See Bryan Magee, *The Story of Philosophy* (London: Dorling Kindersley, 2001), pp. 28–9.
13. Anthony Kenny, ed., *The Oxford Illustrated History of Western Philosophy* (Oxford: Oxford University Press, 1994), p. 25.
14. Benson Saler, 'Lévy-Bruhl, Participation, and Rationality', in Jeppe Sinding Jensen and Luther H. Martin, eds, *Rationality and the Study of Religion* (London: Routledge, 2003), pp. 49–50.
15. See John Daniel Dadosky, 'The Sacred as Real: An Analysis of Eliade's Ontology of the Sacred', in *The Structure of Religious Knowing: Encountering the Sacred in Eliade and Lonergan* (Albany: State University of New York Press, 2004), pp. 99–107.
16. *Ontology*, an eighteenth-century term coming from the Latin *ontologia* and the Greek *òn, ont* (being), is the branch of metaphysics that deals with the nature of being.
17. Mircea Eliade, *The Myth of the Eternal Return: Cosmos and History* (London: Arkana, 1989), pp. xi, 4–5, 35.
18. Robin Horton, 'Lévy-Bruhl, Durkheim and the Scientific Revolution', in Robin Horton and Ruth Finnigan, eds, *Modes of Thought* (London: Faber, 1973), p. 257.
19. Tambiah, *Magic, Science, Religion*, pp. 105–10.
20. Tambiah, *Magic, Science, Religion*, p. 109.
21. Tambiah, *Magic, Science, Religion*, pp. 105–10.
22. Tambiah, *Magic, Science, Religion*, p. 108.

## FURTHER READING

Tambiah, Stanley, 'Multiple Orderings of Reality: The Debate Initiated by Lévy-Bruhl', in *Magic, Science, Religion, and the Scope of Rationality*, Cambridge: Cambridge University Press, 1991, pp. 84–110.

# 3 MAGICAL CONNECTIONS AND ASSOCIATIONS

Some American undergraduate student participants of a psychological experiment watched as two empty, clean bottles were filled with sugar powder poured from a commercially labelled sugar box. The participants were then given two labels, one with 'sucrose' written on it and the other labelled with 'sodium cyanide—poison'. Participants were instructed to attach one label to each bottle, as they preferred. After powder from each bottle was stirred into a separate glass of water, participants were asked to rate their willingness to take a sip from each glass and then to do so. Many were reluctant to drink from the glass with the cyanide-labelled sugar in it, and there was significant preference for the sugar-labelled bottle. The participants acknowledged that their negative feelings toward the poison label were unfounded, as they knew there was only sugar in both glasses. However, in a subsequent study, it was shown that this similarity-based rejection occurred even if the 'cyanide' bottle was labelled 'not sodium cyanide—not poison'. The association had been made by the students—sugar, water and poison were connected in their minds, and even though they knew logically that they would not be poisoned if they drank the 'poison' solution, a magical association had been created, and most avoided it. This is sympathetic magic, a form of associative thought that we use in modern Western societies, even if we do not believe in magic. Notions of magic may exist at different levels of awareness and explicitness, depending on the individual, situational and cultural contexts. Magic 'may be a particularly natural and intuitive mode of thought'.[1]

In this sugar-poison experiment, psychologists Carol Nemeroff and Paul Rozin revised Frazer's classical notion of sympathetic magic to show that far from dying out, magic is very much a part and parcel of modern Western life. They studied sympathetic magic through the observation of Americans subjected to disgusting stimuli, finding that sympathetic magic was at work in the thinking of educated Western adults. They explored the assumption that the name of an entity carries its very nature within it; the name or image equals the referent or object.[2] The magical power of words, as associative thinking, links like with like.

Contagious magic through actual physical contact—direct or indirect—is based on the concept of *isomorphism*: the notion that part is equivalent to the whole; even a very brief contact is capable of transmitting substantial effects, and any part. Nemeroff and Rozin give examples: all parts of Hitler—from his heart to his fingernails—are seen to be equally evil and can transmit evil. This negative contagion is widespread and can be seen in India, where contact with a lower caste is seen as polluting, although there is no enhancement effect of contact with a higher caste (although milk, urine and dung can be used as purifiers because cows are viewed as lower-order deities). On the other hand, positive contagion can be seen embodied in special people such as Mother Theresa and Princess Diana.

American undergraduates, on average, showed substantially stronger contagion effects for objects, such as sweaters, hairbrushes or food, that have been in contact with negative interpersonal sources, for example with an unsavoury person or a disliked individual, than for objects that had contacted positive sources such as friends or lovers. Virtually all participants showed negative contagion effects, but only one-third showed positive contagion effects,[3] even when allowed to select their own personalized positive source person.

How can we further understand what appears to be this natural and intuitive mode of thought? The concept of participation has been a key to our understanding of magic so far, but there are other theories that can also aid knowledge of the processes of the human mind when it thinks magically. In this chapter, we will look at two keys to unlock the theoretical mysteries of magic: sympathetic magic (the association of ideas, as in the preceding example of the poison experiment) and magical analogy (the evocative transference of sets of relationships).

## SYMPATHETIC MAGIC

James Frazer was a classical philosopher and one of the founders of contemporary anthropology. He was born on 1 January 1854 to a devout Presbyterian family in Glasgow. He studied classics, ancient philosophy and law. Later in life, Frazer's interests turned to anthropology, when, at Cambridge, he met William Robertson-Smith, a professor of Arabic. Smith encouraged Frazer to study religious cultures and their rituals. Frazer was also influenced by E. B. Tylor's *Primitive Culture*, which had been published in 1871. Frazer was one of the first to study religion as a social activity that could be examined, rather than the previous tendency to study the truth inherent in various religious claims. Frazer published the first edition of *The Golden Bough* in 1890 to describe a ritual that took place in a sacred grove dedicated to Diana, the Roman huntress goddess, in Nemi, Italy (this will be discussed in Chapter 5 in relation to mythology being a language of magic). The following year, an expanded edition of the book sought to compare similar European rites, drawing parallels between ritual practices in early Christianity and the non-European world. The work was later published in an abridged form in 1921. It is unclear whether Frazer was being antireligious or if he was expressing a subtle version of his own Christian faith. Frazer had his critics, who accused him of being an armchair anthropologist, relying on the accounts of others (including missionaries, with whom he regularly corresponded) and with no direct experience. He has been accused of selecting indiscriminately from different types of cultures, creating a 'Frankenstein's monster with a right eye from Fiji, a left from Europe, one leg from Tierra del Fuego, and one from Tahiti, and all the fingers and toes from still different regions'. Such a figure does not correspond to reality in the past or the present.[4] Nevertheless, Frazer's work has been widely influential, not only to anthropologists such as Bronislaw Malinowski, but also to psychologist Sigmund Freud and poet T. S. Eliot. Frazer died on 7 May 1941, following years of near-blindness.[5]

Magical thinking for Frazer was based on an association of ideas concerning the life, death and rebirth of the cycles of nature, and he coined the term *sympathetic magic* to describe a psychic process underlying this association. *The Golden Bough* (1921) is a mine of myths and stories from cultures all over the world that demonstrate the principles of associative magical thought. Frazer thought that 'things act on each other at a distance through a secret sympathy, the impulse being transmitted from one to the other by means of what we may conceive as a kind of invisible ether'.[6] Frazer's purpose was to prove that magic was a mistaken mode of thinking—'magic is a spurious system of natural law as well as a fallacious guide of conduct; it is a false science as well as an abortive art'[7]—and his exploration of mythological stories and folklore was an evolutionary journey from what he considered to be mistaken magical thought, which turned into religion, towards the truth of science. However, contrary to what Frazer thought, we can find the presence of magic, religion and science simultaneously in modern Western societies and in the thinking of individuals within these societies. People often blend scientific with magical thinking, as the sugar-poison experiment shows.

For Frazer, the human mind that thinks magically employs two different misapplications of sympathetic magic: *homeopathic* magic was founded on the association of ideas by similarity, whereas *contagious* magic was based on the association of ideas by contiguity—the assumption that things that have once been in contact with each other are always in contact. These are the two related aspects of sympathetic magic:

| Homeopathic Magic | Contagious Magic |
|---|---|
| Association by similarity | Association by contiguity |
| Like produces like | Once in contact, always in contact |

Homoeopathic magic was based on what Frazer called the *law of similarity*—the notion that things that resemble each other were the same, and that like produces like or that an effect resembles its cause. This led a magician to infer that it was possible to produce any effect merely by imitating it. Perhaps the most familiar application of this principle, Frazer thought, was the attempt that has been made by many peoples in many ages to injure or destroy an enemy by injuring or destroying an image of that enemy in the belief that just as the image suffers, so does the person, and that when it perishes, the person must die. Frazer pointed to a wide diffusion of this practice all over the world—it was a principle known to sorcerers of ancient India, Babylon and Egypt as well as those of Greece and Rome.

The North American Indians believed that by drawing the figure of a person they wished dead in sand, ashes or clay, or by considering any object as his body, and then by pricking it with a sharp stick or doing it any other injury, they could inflict a corresponding injury on the person represented. Frazer noted that when an Ojebway Indian 'desires to work evil on any one, he makes a little wooden image of his enemy and runs a needle into its head or heart, or he shoots an arrow into it, believing that wherever the needle pierces or the arrow strikes the image, his foe will the same instant be seized with a sharp pain in the corresponding part of his body; but if he intends to kill the person outright, he burns or buries the puppet, uttering certain magic words as he does so'.[8]

The second misapplication of sympathetic magic was contagious magic, the association of ideas by contiguity. Contagious magic was concerned with the law of contact, or contagion, between things which have been in contact; these things continue to act on each other at a distance, after the physical contact has been severed. Whatever is done to a material object will affect equally the person with whom the object was at one time in contact, whether it formed part of the person's body or not. By injuring footprints, you injure the feet that made them. Natives of south-eastern Australia think that they can lame a man by placing sharp pieces of quartz, glass, bone or charcoal in his footprints; the magical virtues of these sharp things enter the body and cause sharp pains. This is what Lévy-Bruhl termed *pars pro toto*—the notion that the part is equivalent to the whole, as we saw in one of his examples of participation in Chapter 2.

Another example of contagious magic is menstruation, which is seen to have great potency and power. Menstruation has been subject to symbolic elaboration in a wide variety of cultures and has been studied by anthropologists as taboo (a supernaturally sanctioned law) and pollution (a symbolic contamination). Menstrual taboos have been seen as evidence of primitive irrationality, and a wide range of distinct rules for conduct regarding menstruation is found cross-culturally.[9] Menstrual blood is used in love charms and potions, as in this fictional conversation in southern Illinois:

"You remember your Uncle Skinny and your Aunt Jac, don't you?"

"Yes, ma'am," Ward said. "I remember them pretty well."

"Maybe you don't remember this, but your Uncle Skinny snuck around on your aunt a lot. That is, till she come to me, said that Skinny was stepping out on her, said she wanted to keep him at home. So I told her to put a spoonful of her 'time of the month' in his coffee regularly. If she did, he'd never leave her. Of course, you know what happened, I'm sure. Your uncle died in your aunt's arms, loving her to the very end."

Ward was shocked to hear the tale, but he remembered his Uncle Skinny's often docile, loving manner toward his Aunt Jac.[10]

Menstrual blood is sometimes used ritually with the negative intent of bringing harm to others, especially through witchcraft. Among the Mae Enga, it is held that menstrual blood put into a man's food will kill him, while in China, menstrual blood is said to adhere to the ground, making it dangerous to walk on the streets.[11]

Much magic combines homeopathic and contagious magic, as in the case of a person creating a likeness doll of the person he wants to harm (homeopathic magic) and then adding hair, nail clippings or perhaps a piece of that person's clothing (contagious magic), as also in the example of the sugar-poison experiment at the beginning of this chapter. In this case, the student participants associated the sugar water with poison in their minds through the law of similarity—the words *sugar* and *poison* took on a similarity. The law of contact operated through the placing of the sugar water in bottles labelled 'sodium cyanide'; the words *sodium cyanide* induced contagious magic, even when the label was altered to read 'not sodium cyanide—not poison'. The students knew that they could not actually be poisoned, but there was an intuitive psychological link that most were reluctant to ignore.

### Magic into Science

A writer of his time, Frazer embraced the then current evolutionary ideas; he thought that there was a movement of higher thought from magic through religion to science. Frazer thought that science had much in common with magic—both rested on a faith in order as the underlying principle of all things—but that differences resulted from the mode in which the two orders had been reached. Magic reckoned on an extension by false analogy of ideas that were presented to the mind, whereas science was derived from patient and exact observation of phenomena. The future lies with science:

Here at last, after groping about in the dark for countless ages, man has hit upon a clue to the labyrinth, a golden key that opens many locks in the treasury of nature. It is probably not too much to say that the hope of progress—moral and intellectual as well as material—in the future is bound up with the fortunes of science, and that every obstacle placed in the way of scientific discovery is a wrong to humanity.[12]

Frazer saw sympathetic magic as mistaken thinking, a mode of thought that would ultimately give way to science as a superior theory. Indeed, he wrote that in the last analysis, 'as science has supplanted its predecessors, so it may hereafter be itself superseded by some more perfect hypothesis, perhaps by some totally different way of looking at the phenomena—of registering the shadows on the screen—of which we in this generation can form no idea'.[13]

For Frazer, 'the fatal flaw of magic' lay in the mistaken applications of the association of ideas inherent in sympathetic magic. He noted that the principles of association were excellent in themselves and were 'absolutely essential to the working of the human mind', but legitimately applied, they yielded science, and illegitimately applied, they yielded magic, which he called the 'bastard sister of science'. For Frazer, all magic was necessarily false and barren, 'for were it ever to become true and fruitful, it would no longer be magic but science':

> From the earliest times man has been engaged in a search for general rules whereby to turn the order of natural phenomena to his own advantage, and in the long search he has scraped together a great hoard of such maxims, some of them golden and some of them mere dross. The true or golden rules constitute the body of applied science which we call the arts; the false are magic.[14]

Magic is not simply the result of erroneous thinking; indeed, magic shaped the historical development of the scientific experimental method. Contrary to what Frazer thought, magic did not give way to religion and science; rather, the practical and experimental aspects of magic were adopted by science, and many of the ideas inherent in sympathetic magic were absorbed. One figure associated with the change from speculation to experiment was Francis Bacon (1561–1626), a philosopher of science and a statesman to Queen Elizabeth I, who wanted to transform the investigation of the natural world. Although Bacon was highly critical of sympathetic magic, he valued its empirical method and was concerned to know how knowledge was justified, how it could be expanded and how it could be made useful; he was not interested with discoveries, but rather, with the nature of science itself.[15]

There was nothing irrational in Bacon's day in believing in magic; the belief that bodies had specific properties that enabled them to act upon or interact with other bodies to bring about particular ends entirely conformed to rational beliefs in corresponding planes along the Great Chain of Being (the hierarchical scheme whereby God created the world according to his grand plan); there was a logic behind any claims about sympathies.[16] It was the multiplex of correspondences between different links in the Great Chain of Being that underwrote sympathetic magic; the magician exploited the sympathies and the antipathies between things and brought them together or separated them. In his *New Abecedarium of Nature*, Bacon wrote, 'We must . . . investigate the individual and particular friendships and quarrels or sympathies and antipathies of bodies with diligence and care, seeing that they bring with them such a number of useful things.'[17] The art of magic was not in understanding nature, but to put its powers to use; the whole point of magic was to exploit natural phenomena, the natural powers of bodies and their forces and movements, to bring about practical ends, and its principal method was experimental.[18]

However, the experimental process was complicated—experimental evidence has to be interpreted, and interpretations tend to fit into preconceived expectations and assumptions, and these often obscure alternative possibilities. Take for example the case of the weapon salve, a magical ointment developed and promoted by the Paracelsians (followers of Paracelsus, 1493–1541, a Swiss physician, alchemist and astrologer). It could cure wounds incurred in battle by the application of the ointment to the weapon that caused the wound. If the weapon was not available, then the ointment was applied to a bandage or piece of cloth that had been soaked in blood from the wound but which was then kept away from the injury. This was a practical application of sympathetic magic—by applying the ointment to the weapon, a connection between the healing ointment, the weapon and the injured was created through sympathetic magic.

This proved to be much more successful than the usual means of treating wounds because the standard method of treatment was based on the medical theory of laudable pus, a notion that pus was a good and healing reaction of the body. These were the days before antiseptics, the knowledge of invisible germs and the need for hygiene. It was thought that the formation of pus in a wound was part of the healing process, a conclusion based on observational evidence. Doctors and surgeons would pack wounds with irritating substances, such as ground eggshells, sand and coarse feathers, to stimulate the formation of pus. 'In the case of serious wounds they would often bandage the packed wound really tightly to increase the irritation, and would arrange a goose quill (or some other tube), emerging from the dressing, to act as an outlet pipe to drain off the pus as it formed.'[19] It is obvious to us, with the benefit of what we now know about hygiene, that the experimental evidence was on the side of magic. The theory of laudable pus was so strongly held that it was concluded that the weapon salve had an occult power of curing wounds without the formation of pus, not that the theory of laudable pus was wrong. It took a long time to sort this out and arrive at the real truth of the matter.

Much magic was combined with aspects of natural philosophy to give rise to something closer to modern science. However, magic always threatened religious authorities, and during the process of amalgamation, magic was seldom, if ever, acknowledged: 'the good ideas in magic were silently incorporated into the reformed natural knowledge, while the bad ideas were used, more and more vigorously, to denounce magic as a sink of false and ludicrous beliefs.'[20] Magic increasingly came to be seen as concerned with a supernatural realm in which only the superstitious believed.[21] This is the context in which Frazer could come to write that magic was a spurious system of natural law and a false science. Notwithstanding the co-option of various elements of magic, it did not disappear, as the sugar-poison experiment mentioned earlier demonstrates. This is due to the fact that magic, as an aspect of mind, is universal to human beings.

Despite his negative views of magic in relation to science, Frazer's ideas about magical associative thought are helpful in understanding how participation works though connections and relationships with phenomena. Another useful theory that can help us understand the experience of magic is analogical thinking.

## ANALOGICAL THINKING

Whereas Frazer's sympathetic magic makes associations between things through notions of similarity or contagion, magical analogical thinking is a type of logic that connects one thing as it takes on the qualities of another. We can take Frazer's description of a Bengali prince as an analogical example. The prince planted a tree in the courtyard of his father's palace before he went away to a far country, and he said to his parents, 'This tree is my life. When you see the tree green and fresh, then know that it is well with me; when you see the tree fade in some parts, then know that I am in an ill case; and when you see the whole tree fade, then you know that I am dead and gone.'[22] In this world, all is connected; this is a perspective that is still held by many peoples. Sometimes it is the souls of the dead which are believed to animate trees. Frazer explains that the Dieri tribe of central Australia regard as very sacred certain trees which are supposed to be their fathers transformed; hence they speak with reverence of these trees and are careful that they are not cut down or burned.[23]

Another example of analogy is provided by early-twentieth-century American anthropologist Ruth Benedict, who views reasoning by analogy as universal and takes philosopher and historian Oswald Spengler's *Decline of the West* (1918), a treatise on the cyclical nature of the rise and decline of civilizations, as her example. Spengler's work, which had an influence on William S. Burroughs, Jack Kerouac and Allen Ginsberg of the beat generation (a group of radical American writers in the 1950s), showed how patternings of civilisations were analogous to the birth-death cycle of living organisms in the manner in which they progressed from youth through their prime and then into old age. Spengler outlined two great destiny ideas—the classical Apollonian and the modern Faustian world views—both based on myth. These two views of destiny are outlined in the following table:

| Apollonian World View of Destiny | Faustian World View of Destiny |
|---|---|
| Soul = ordered cosmos | A force endlessly combating obstacles |
| Conflict is evil | Inner development |
| Life is threatened from outside | Catastrophes of existence come as an inevitable culmination of past choices and experiences |
| | Conflict is the essence of existence |
| | Reaches outwards to the infinite |

Benedict is mindful of the problems of treating modern, stratified societies as if they had homogeneity, but the two models do provide us with a good exposition of analogical thinking—how one thing (be it Apollonian or Faustian myth) is modelled on another (the organic life-death cycle). Having gained some sense of analogy, we can now turn to its specific use in magical thinking. In this regard, analogical thinking is particularly associated with the work of anthropologist Stanley Jeyaraja Tambiah.

## Persuasive Analogy

Stanley Jeyaraja Tambiah was born on 16 January 1929 in Sri Lanka to a Christian Tamil family and was educated to undergraduate level at the University of Ceylon. After going to Cornell University in the United States to gain his doctorate in 1954, he returned to teach at the University of Ceylon. He has since been Professor of Anthropology at the Universities of Cambridge (from 1963 to 1972), the University of Chicago (from 1973 to 1976) and Harvard University (from 1973 until the present). Tambiah's work has concentrated on Buddhism and its political relationships in Thailand, Sri Lanka and other areas. Working on an ethnohistorical study of modern and medieval Thailand, he became interested in the study of Western thought, in particular, the manner in which anthropologists used the conceptual categories of magic, science and religion to make sense of other cultures.[24] The issues discussed in his book *Magic, Science, Religion, and the Scope of Rationality*, published in 1991, stimulate reflection on the status of social reality and particularly the investigation of it by science. Tambiah's work is important for a study of magic because it makes us question our everyday assumptions about the categories of understandings we use—the terms *magic, science* and *religion* are heavily loaded and mean different things for different people.

Tambiah's starting point in his earlier paper 'The Form and Meaning of Magical Acts' is to study the different ways that analogies can be used.[25] As we have already seen, an analogy is an agreement or similarity between things, and analogical thinking is a type of reasoning based on analogy. A connection is made between things that are like one another in the experience of the person making the connection. Analogical thinking organizes experiences into meaningful patterns whereby the meaning has individual significance, and it is based on magical, rather than causal, connections. Analogy depends on the recognition of similarities between instances compared or experienced. Tambiah shows how it is inappropriate to compare magic with science. Both science and magic work by virtue of analogy, but different types of analogy: science is based in empiricism and seeks validity through the scientific method, whereas magic works to persuade—it is always accompanied by performative speech seeking to make change in the world. Thus both magic and science use analogical thought; this mode of thinking underlies science as well as magical spells and rituals.

Scientific analogy depends on the causal relationship between objects and their qualities. Predictions can be made from known sets of causal relationships to similar but unknown sets so that empirically verifiable hypotheses and comparisons can be generated. In this scientific perspective, the known instance serves as a model for the incompletely known: the model serves as a prediction concerning the explanation, which is then subject to observation and test. Whereas *persuasive analogy* is a set of analogical relationships based on magic. Magical analogies connect with an alternative mode of reality that is more than just the observable material world—the associations are magical, rather than scientific:

| Scientific Analogy | Persuasive Analogy |
|---|---|
| Causal relationship between objects and their qualities | Magical relationship between phenomena |
| Known instance serves as a model for the incompletely known | Transfer of qualities through sympathetic magic |
|  | Employed during ritual and spells |

Magical analogy involves an evocative transference of the value or meaning implied on one set of relationships to a second set of relationships. For example Bronislaw Malinowski, in his classic fieldwork study of Trobriand coral gardens, claimed that magic formed a sacred language that was used for a different purpose to everyday language. Spells formed a magical system that could not be understood by ordinary criteria of grammar, logic and consistency but could be understood through magical analogy.

Malinowski had observed that most magic was chanted in a form of sing-song and that it was profoundly different from ordinary utterances[26]: a magician recites spells in a rhythmic, metaphorical and alliterative manner with 'weird cadences and repetitions'. The words do not have meaning in any ordinary sense. Malinowski described magic as happening in a world of its own that was real to natives, and also had to be real to anthropologists because the magic had a deep influence on behaviour and so had to be taken seriously. Acts of magic were performances for the production and conveyance of a magical force. This magic, which existed from the beginning of time and was a universal language acquired in infancy, resided in spells as primeval texts that came into being with animals, plants, winds, waves, human diseases, human courage and human frailty. When magical spells were used, the words exercised a power by virtue of their primeval, mysterious connection with an esoteric aspect of this reality. The spells express an esoteric meaning that is created through analogy. For example a dolphin is big and long as the tubers should become; its weaving in and out of the rising and falling waves is associated with the winding and interweaving of the luxuriant vines whose rich foliage means a plentiful *taytu* harvest. Likewise, the bush hen's large nest is associated with the swelling, round *taytu* plant when tubers are plentiful[27]—as the bush hen's nest is large, so the tubers will become large.

Another example of persuasive analogical thinking is provided in the prayer (*mönlam*) of Kuntu Sangpo, a Tibetan tantric deity, a symbolic representation of a universal, all-pervasive primal space. Tantric (*vajrayana*) rituals aim to achieve enlightenment or to bring effects within everyday reality such as long life and health.[28] Tibetan Buddhist practitioners can recite the prayer and meditate on Kuntu Sangpo and take on his qualities through a transfer of meaning. Kuntu Sangpo, as a deity, represents a mode of reality that human beings and other sentient beings—such as gods, animals, hell beings and so on—are thought to be capable of experiencing:

> HO! The phenomenal world and all existence, *samsara* and *nirvana*,
> All has one foundation, but there are two paths and two results—
> Displays of both ignorance and Knowledge.
> Through Kuntu Sangpo's aspiration,
> In the Palace of the Primal Space of Emptiness
> Let all beings attain perfect consummation and Buddhahood.
>
> The universal foundation is unconditioned,
> Spontaneously arising, a vast immanent expanse, beyond expression,
> Where neither 'samsara' nor 'nirvana' exist.
> Knowledge of this reality is Buddhahood,
> While ignorant beings wander in *samsara*.
> Let all sentient beings of the three realms
> Attain Knowledge of the nature of the ineffable foundation.[29]

The essential process is the analogic transmission of one quality to another, a shift from one mode of reality to another through passion that dissolves stress and allows release into the universal foundation.[30] Analogic shifts such as this are central to all *vajrayana* (shamanic tantric) rituals, the purpose of which may be to attain Buddhahood, as in the ritual quoted, or to achieve good health and long life. In reciting the prayer and doing the meditation, they are conceiving of themselves as Kuntu Sangpo, and, through the analogical shift, take on his qualities—the aim being a magical connection through passion and images, rather than logical and intellectual reasoning.

For Tambiah, the empirical mode of science and the persuasive, performative mode of ritual magic represent two types of thought, and the criteria of the one should not be applied to the other. Tambiah has pointed out that the analogical relation and the wished-for effect are stated verbally with the homeopathic act. However, for him, this is more than just 'like attracts like'; it engages similarities (positive analogies) and differences (negative analogies). These are judged by different standards that have the objectives of persuasion, conceptualization and expansion of meaning.[31] The expansion of meaning is understood through magical consciousness.

Thus it can be seen that sympathetic magic and persuasive analogical thinking are examples of theories that attempt to explain the manner in which magical consciousness operates through associations and connections, as shown in the following table:

| **Sympathetic Magic** | **Persuasive Analogy** |
|---|---|
| The association of ideas by similarity or by contact | The transference of value or meaning according to magical association, e.g. spells |

In the next chapter, we will see how important these principles are to the experience of magic.

## NOTES

1. Carol Nemeroff and Paul Rozin, 'The Makings of the Magical Mind: The Nature and Function of Sympathetic Magical Thinking', in Karl S. Rosengren, Carl N. Johnson and Paul L. Harris, eds, *Imagining the Impossible: Magical, Scientific, and Religious Thinking in Children* (Cambridge: Cambridge University Press, 2000), pp. 5–7, 25.

2. In P. Rozin, L. Millman and C. Nemeroff, 'Operation of the Laws of Sympathetic Magic in Disgust and Other Domains', *Journal of Personality and Social Psychology*, SO (1986), pp. 703–12, and P. Rozin, M. Markwith and B. Ross, 'The Sympathetic Magical Law of Similarity, Nominal

Realism, and Neglect of Negatives in Response to Negative Labels', *Psychological Science*, 1 (1990), pp. 383–4.

3. C. Nemeroff and P. Rozin, 'The Contagion Concept in Adult Thinking in the United States: Transmission of Germs and of Interpersonal Influence', *Ethos*, 22 (1994), pp. 158–86; P. Rozin, C. Nemeroff, M. Wane and A. Sherrod, 'Operation of the Sympathetic Magical Law of Contagion in Interpersonal Attitudes among Americans', *Bulletin of the Psychonomic Society*, 27 (1989), pp. 27, 367–70.

4. Ruth Benedict, *Patterns of Culture* (New York: Mentor Books, 1948), p. 44.

5. 'James George Frazer', http://www.giffordlectures.org/Author.asp?AuthorID=67, accessed 13 March 2009.

6. James Frazer, *The Golden Bough: A Study in Magic and Religion* (Ware: Wordsworth, 1993), p. 12.

7. Frazer, *The Golden Bough*, pp. 11–12.

8. Frazer, *The Golden Bough*, p. 13.

9. Thomas Buckley and Alma Gottlieb, 'A Critical Appraisal of Theories of Menstrual Symbolism', in Thomas Buckley and Alma Gottlieb, eds, *Blood Magic: The Anthropology of Menstruation* (Berkeley: University of California Press, 1988), pp. 3–4.

10. Matthew Kirksey Dying, *Grassroots 1984*, quoted in Buckley and Gottlieb, *Blood Magic*, p. 35.

11. Buckley and Gottlieb, *Blood Magic*, pp. 34–5.

12. Frazer, *Golden Bough*, pp. 711–12.

13. Frazer, *Golden Bough*.

14. Frazer, *Golden Bough*, p. 50.

15. John Henry, *Knowledge Is Power: How Magic, the Government and an Apocalyptic Vision Inspired Francis Bacon to Create Modern Science* (Cambridge: Icon Books, 2002), pp. 1–3.

16. Henry, *Knowledge Is Power*, pp. 69–71.

17. Henry, *Knowledge Is Power*, pp. 44–5.

18. Henry, *Knowledge Is Power*, pp. 44–53.

19. Henry, *Knowledge Is Power*, p. 77.

20. Henry, *Knowledge Is Power*, p. 79.

21. Henry, *Knowledge Is Power*, pp. 78–80.

22. Frazer, *Golden Bough*, p. 670.

23. Frazer, *Golden Bough*, p. 115.

24. 'Stanley Tambiah', http://www.mnsu.edu/emuseum/information/biography/pqrst/tambiah_stanley. html, accessed 13 March 2009.

25. Stanley Tambiah, 'The Form and Meaning of Magical Acts: A Point of View', in William A. Lessa and Evon Z. Vogt, eds, *Reader in Comparative Religion: An Anthropological Approach*, 4th ed. (New York: Harper and Row, 1979), pp. 352–3; originally published in Robin Horton and Ruth Finnegan, eds, *Modes of Thought* (London: Faber and Faber, 1973), pp. 199–229; also as Chapter 2 in Stanley Tambiah, *Culture, Thought, and Social Action* (Cambridge, MA: Harvard University Press, 1985).

26. Bronislaw Malinowski, *Coral Gardens and Their Magic* (New York: Dover, 1978), p. 233.

27. Bronislaw Malinowski, 'The Meaning of Meaningless Words and the Coefficient of Weirdness', in *Coral Gardens*, pp. 213–22; for an online version, see http://www.ubu.com/ethno/discourses/malin. html, accessed 13 March 2009.

28. Geoffrey Samuel, *Civilized Shamans: Buddhism in Tibetan Societies* (Washington, DC: Smithsonian Institution Press, 1993), p. 9.

29. Keith Dowman, *The Aspiration of Kuntuzangpo* (Kathmandu: Diamond Sow, 1981), p. 4; cited in Samuel, *Civilized Shamans*, pp. 13–14.

30. Samuel, *Civilized Shamans*, pp. 13–16.

31. Tambiah, *Culture, Thought, and Social Action*.

## FURTHER READING

Nemeroff, Carol, and Paul Rozin, 'The Makings of the Magical Mind: The Nature and Function of Sympathetic Magical Thinking', in Karl S. Rosengren, Carl N. Johnson and Paul L. Harris, eds, *Imagining the Impossible: Magical, Scientific, and Religious Thinking in Children* (Cambridge: Cambridge University Press, 2000), pp. 1–34.

Tambiah, Stanley, *Culture, Thought, and Social Action* (Cambridge, MA: Harvard University Press, 1985).

# SECTION TWO
# THE EXPERIENCE OF MAGIC

Being an anthropologist in such a research situation has been an uncomfortable process; it has involved self-examination and exploration, often in a confrontation with fear; but it has been conducted within a broader commitment to further understanding and communication.[1]

—Susan Greenwood

Talking now we're in this space of creative possibility. Don't try to stop it or measure it (I'm getting a sense of a ruler). I have to put rules and regulations aside to step into the centre of it. You can feel it. It's multidimensional, above, below, by the side; another layer.[2]

—Jo Crow

Using my own experience, in this section, I focus on breaking down the barrier between researcher and researched to show how magical consciousness flows through emotion and the mythological imagination.

# 4 MAGICAL CONSCIOUSNESS

'If you look through a holed stone—a witch's stone—you get a different perspective'.
Jo Crow, a British shaman, and I were standing on the beach at Hope Gap, Seaford
Head, in England, on a balmy but cloudy autumnal October day. The sun was peep-
ing through the clouds to light up one or two of the Seven Sisters, seven of the white
cliffs so characteristic of Sussex's chalk downland. I had picked up a sandy-coloured
holed stone striped with black. I placed it back on the beach, and Jo picked it up and
looked through it. Some time later, she pressed another stone into my hand, saying,
'Feel that.' As I felt the two smooth sides cold in my hand, I looked down and saw
that it was a fossilized sea urchin. Fossils such as this are not rare on this beach, but
they can be extremely difficult to find. 'They find you,' Jo said. She had used the tiger
stone to look through to find the fossil. When in this state of consciousness, the stones
come to you. It is a question of shifting awareness. This experience with the holed
witch's stone can be understood through the concept of magical consciousness—by
connecting with the stone and focusing her attention, the fossil came to Jo. She had
'opened up her heart' to feel the emotion, to feel the connection and to direct the intent through the holed stone. In this chapter, we will examine magical consciousness
as an affective awareness experienced through an alternative mode of mind.

## A PLIABLE MENTAL SPACE

Lévy-Bruhl emphasised the social dimensions of participation, but what has concerned
me are the individual and psychological aspects of magical experience. A central part
of this experience is the ability to use the imagination, and this is not just the preserve
of mystical thought—the mind is adaptive and constantly creative, as shown in the
work of English neurologist Oliver Sacks (1933–). Described as a neuroanthropologist
because he uses clinical tales and anecdotes, rather than the dry case histories reported
in conventional medical textbooks, Sacks tells stories about his patients' experiences.
Restoring the narrative of experience to science, he has reenvisioned the mind from
the Western biomedical model of a passive, ghostly decoder of stimuli to an interac-
tive, adaptive and endlessly innovative participant in the creation of the world.

Sacks argues that the brain has almost unlimited plasticity; when the human organism is faced with a new situation, it must adapt, for example deafness and the use of sign language lead to an enhancement of perception and visual intelligence. The denial of one sense can totally reshape our perception of the world—defects, disorders and diseases such as colour-blindness, deafness and blindness can act as creative forces on the neurological system by bringing out latent powers and developments. When it comes to the brain, they may force it to make other neuronal paths to compensate for the damaged or diseased part. Showing how his patients strive for identity in a world utterly deranged by their disorders, he describes patients living with Tourette's syndrome, autism, Parkinsonism, schizophrenia and Alzheimer's disease and demonstrates how they survive and adapt to these different neurological diseases. In the process, Sacks explores what this can tell us about the human mind.[3]

The following example shows the importance of a pliable and responsive mind. Australian psychologist Zoltan Torey, author of *The Crucible of Consciousness* (1999), was blinded at the age of twenty-one whilst working in a chemical factory. After this accident, Torey resolved to develop his inner eye and the powers of visual imagery by generating, holding and then manipulating images in his mind. Torey constructed imagined visual worlds as a sort of controlled dream, and this enabled him to replace the guttering on his roof. As he explained, 'I replaced the entire roof guttering of my multi-gabled home single-handed . . . and solely on the strength of the accurate and well-focused manipulation of my now totally pliable and responsive mental space.'[4] Torey later explained to Sacks that his neighbours were greatly alarmed at seeing a blind man alone at night in pitch darkness on his roof. Sacks notes that Torey's blindness had enabled him to think in ways that had not been available to him before, 'to envisage solutions, models, designs, to project himself to the inside of machines and other systems, and, finally, to grasp by visual thought and simulation (complemented by all the data of neuroscience) the complexities of that ultimate system, the human brain-mind'.[5]

How could Torey do this? Torey's father, Sacks explains, was the head of a large motion picture studio and would give his son scripts to read. This enabled him to visualize stories, plots and characters, to work with his imagination. Torey also maintained a cautious and scientific attitude to his visual imagery, checking the accuracy of images before risking his life to replace the guttering on his roof. For example, he used to imagine and visualize the inside of a differential gearbox in action as if from inside its casing. The powers of the imagination dissolve and transform, unify and create, drawing on memory and association.[6] Sacks demonstrated how imagined visual worlds could occur through the manipulation of a pliable mental space as a so-called controlled dream. It is possible to imagine oneself inside a machine to develop a logical knowledge of how a gearbox works; this can be imaginatively compared to the structure of an atom or a cell.

This controlled dream–like thinking, as demonstrated in the example of Zoltan Torey, requires the flexibility of a pliable mental space, one that is able to range freely beyond the usual constrictions of everyday thinking. Looking at it analytically, the senses can be constantly developed and expanded by the imagination, in combination with developing the inner eye and the powers of visual imagery as well as the other senses of hearing, touch, taste and smell. Using my fieldwork with shaman Jo Crow, I will show how this pliable mental space is also used in magical consciousness to connect with an inspirited dimension of material reality through emotion and feeling with the heart.

## A PLACE OF LIMITLESS POSSIBILITY

A modern-day shaman with hair in silver dreadlocks decorated with beads and plaited ribbons, Jo lives what seems like an ordinary life. Now in her fifties, she has three children, many grandchildren and a partner—but she is not ordinary in an everyday sense because, as a shaman, she is in communication with a spirit world, and she is a healer. I was aware of Jo when I was first researching magic in the early 1990s; she was a friend of a friend, and I used to see her at pagan gatherings in London from time to time. We got to know each other after we met at another mutual friend's house. I thought she had some interesting views and asked her if I could interview her for my research. She agreed, and we eventually met up when I visited her at home some time later.

We have had the opportunity to talk at length on numerous occasions since about various issues to do with magic. On one such occasion, I was sitting on her living room carpet, and Jo, relaxed on the sofa, went into a light trance to explain her view of magic:

> Talking now we're in this space of creative possibility. Don't try to stop it or measure it (I'm getting a sense of a ruler). I have to put rules and regulations aside to step into the centre of it. You can feel it. It's multidimensional, above, below, by the side; another layer. Move into this place where it's possible to see threads of connections. It's a suspended place of limitless possibilities— the centre of everywhere and nowhere baby (I'm hearing this song 'Hi Ho Silver Lining' [laughs]). You just suspend yourself there and wait.

This is a place where there are no answers, but opportunities for exploration:

> It's a different way of seeing the world; it's like going deeper into a three-dimensional picture to investigate and play, to swim in the water of possibilities. Let the boundaries go; it's so powerful to 'not know', I can't possibly be wrong: there are no answers, just exploration. You have to relax your logical mind and

trust in not knowing, the minute you try it's like a slippery fish or a bar of soap, and it's gone. Trying to understand stops the flow. It's not a place of facts and figures, it's a place of suspension; the boundaries are limitless . . . I have a picture of logical thinking as a footpath with stepping stones but this way of thinking comes from multi-directions all at once; you can take them through anyway you like. To try and control it is to miss it, to miss the point.

Jo moves through this place in her imagination when she is healing a client; she opens her heart to creative possibilities and 'journeys' to resolve the person's problem:

> When I journey I split into many parts: there's me 'doing'—the strong core of me, my centre; there's me 'over-seeing'; and part of me is dancing to maintain the space, keeping the boundaries open, a gatekeeper; and my physical body that may be dancing or lying on the floor.

Jo's consciousness is split and this shows some of the complexity of working in a magical state of mind. Her consciousness is not unitary—it has many dimensions and it is connected with spirits.

When she was very young, the spirits first started to talk to Jo. She said that conversations occurred in which it was discussed what she would be when she grew up. During one of these conversations, Jo was shown a long pole with a man and the word *shaman* on the top—'like a toy monkey on a stick'. Jo had heard of the word shaman but did not know what it meant: 'there was a kid around the corner called Chrissy Shaman, I thought I'd marry him,' she said. Jo forgot about this for the following years, whilst she was 'busy getting married and having children'. Then many years later, when she was sitting on her sofa reading a tarot book, she saw the word shaman, and she said she nearly fell off the chair in surprise. She meditated, and it all came rolling back 'like a discovery voyage'. The spirits had not gone away—they were the thoughts that joined her in her musings; they were a part of her and she could feel them, particularly at times of crisis.

Subsequently, during a Michael Harner–style shamanic workshop in which participants journeyed in their imaginations to the beat of a drum, she had another experience with the man on the top of the long pole:

> As we started to journey I lay down and I put my drum on my back, I lay on my front and I put my drum on my back, and it felt very strong to do that, not the usual way to do it at all. I journeyed and the four winds came and took me (these four winds I have represented by ribbons on my dance robe). I just went flying, flying across land and sea, mountains, landscapes, tumbling, tumbling, tumbling—really like being tossed about in the wind. All of a sudden I was caught.

There was a man standing right on the top of a pole, he was tied to it, right up high and I went flying and tumbling through the air past him and he grabbed me and held me round the middle and he pushed his face into my face and my heart into his heart and our bellies and everything, torsos, totally tight. And he hung on, and he put his mouth to my mouth I could feel his hot breath wet against my face, he blew and sucked so we breathed together and our hearts beat together. He sucked my breath into him and he blew our breath into me so we exchanged breaths backwards and forwards. Really strong. I could feel this thing happening, all the senses were very strong. He was a Mongolian man and I could smell his clothes, his breath. It was really strong, not very nice at all, quite smelly [laughs].

We drew breath for ages and he said, 'I am you and you are me and now we are together.' I'd read about things like that and I suppose that he was my spirit husband, but I don't know about things like that. We were like one anyway. He said he would be with me and that he would put himself inside my head so that I could connect with him. For quite a while I had this huge cavernous feeling in my head. It's interesting because some people at this thing [the drum workshop] thought that I'd been possessed by spirit and that he had blown himself into me and this was not safe. But it was not like that at all because this is someone who is me, who I have been or am.[7]

This is a good example of spirit participation. The reference to the pole may relate to the 'world pole' as an axis between the different realms negotiated by the shaman; the passage between one cosmic region and another—from earth to sky, and earth to underworld. This is a good example of spirit participation. Communication between different realms is made possible by a central axis that aids interconnections. Many nomadic peoples imagine the sky as a tent, and in the middle of the sky shines the Pole Star, an axis of the world holding the celestial tent like a stake; the Mongols call this the Golden Pillar.[8] This initiation was important; it brought back the conversations with spirits that Jo had had as a child during a traumatic period in her life and she interpreted the man on the pole as an aspect of herself.

## THINKING WITH THE HEART

At the age of thirteen, Jo had an initiation into the spirit world when she underwent major heart surgery. It was this crisis that she says enabled her to think with her heart. During the trauma, she went into a suspended place, where she did not know who she was:

I saw myself as suspended in deep dark space. Everything that was me was ripped away. I was in the void. From that void came slowly these communications came to me as voices, conversations, pictures—what I call 'knowings'.

> I slowly came back down into physical and emotional pain and I spent time
> out floating in the void and it became familiar. Slowly glimmerings—you can
> pick them up—led me back to the centre through threads on the web. From
> the place of void I started to weave my world again.

Gradually she recovered and got on with her everyday life, but she continued to have
experiences through her heart, and she feels the world through her emotions. Emotion induced by this crisis was the catalyst for Jo to create a new pattern of meanings
in her life.

Feeling consciousness through the heart is not specific to Jo Crow. Urgunge Onon,
a Daur Mongol born in Manchuria, northern China, who now lives in England,
also experiences consciousness through his heart. He says that astronomers analyse
the universe through maths and physics but that Daur Mongols do it through their
consciousness, and this consciousness is felt through the heart. In their collaborative
book, Caroline Humphrey describes how Urgunge wanted to explain Daur Mongol
shamanism to Westerners: 'it was when he had become an elder, mettlesome and
every shining black hair in place but approaching the age of seventy, that Urgunge
Onon suggested we explore his memories. He wanted a book to be written about the
shamanism of his youth, a book which would explain shamanism both as an anthropological subject and "from inside"?'.[9]

According to Urgunge, for Daur Mongols, the sky is beyond time, and each
human being has a part of the sky in him. This is his consciousness—it is both at the
centre of each person and far away, out in the cosmos. This universe is coloured, a vast
expanse of blueness, deeper blue the farther away it is, and in the blue there are two
points representing the self: an outer, cosmic one, which is like a bright star in the sky,
and an inner one, which is red. Urgunge Onon feels it like a 'red hole which is nothing but his heart, sensing and alive. It is breathing, pulsating with a barely perceptible
noise. That pulse is his power.'[10] Consciousness leaping outwards gives each person
her own orbit and her own independence—'*ooriin tenggertei, oorinn terguultei*' (your
own sky, your own cart track). The Daur Mongol heart is the centre of consciousness,
and it enables participation with the cosmos. Between a person and the sky is a vast
space where it is possible to fly.[11]

The notion of the centrality of the heart to an analysis of consciousness challenges scientific notions of mind, which are usually understood as originating
from the brain; in Western thought, the mind is associated with the head. The
heart is not just a muscular pump; it is the largest generator of electromagnetic
signals, and it radiates strong fields of energy. The nervous system connects the
brain and heart, and it appears that the heart may have a complex nervous system with neurons that have a short- and long-term memory. The heart's internal

nervous system allows heart transplants between people—the heart remembers how to beat when it is placed in the recipient's chest cavity. The question that some scientists are asking is whether it has a higher-level memory; the memory is not localized, but distributed throughout the whole nervous system. The heart is the most efficient organ in processing emotions; it reacts intuitively and sends messages to the emotional area of the brain via a neural network feedback system.[12] All this suggests that the heart may have mind as well as being the symbolic centre of our emotions; the heart is also at the centre of participation. Consciousness is a whole-body participatory experience. In the case of Jo Crow and Urgunge Onon, it also involves affective relationships with other human beings, and it can extend outwards into the cosmos.

In this regard, the emotional involvement with magic is very different to the explanation put forward by Bronislaw Malinowski.[13] For Malinowski, the function of magic was cathartic—it had an affinity with emotional outbursts, with daydreaming and with unrealizable desire.[14] Magic occurred when there was a gap in practical activities: when a hunter was disappointed by his quarry, or when a sailor missed propitious winds, or when a canoe builder had to deal with some uncertain material or when a healthy person suddenly felt his strength failing.[15] For Malinowski, magic relieves emotional tension—it is a universal psychophysical mechanism, an extended expression of emotion. Malinowski's conception of magic reduces magic to psychological factors that occur in the absence of reason. His mature theory of magic identifies the human capacity for the magical use of language acquired during childhood[16]:

| Malinowski's View of Magic | Magical Consciousness |
| --- | --- |
| Relieves emotional tension<br><br>Psychophysical expression<br><br>Cathartic<br><br>Occurs in the absence of reason and practical knowledge | Creates emotional meaning; a form of associative thinking through sensory patterns of interrelatedness |

By contrast, I want to show how magic is an aspect of mind that occurs through a process of experience. Rather than an emotional reaction that happens in the absence of reason, magic is a creative and pliable place, where it is possible to explore deeper spiritual dimensions of life and death. I have found this to be personally meaningful, as I shall show subsequently.

## PARTICIPATION WITH A SPIRIT HORSE

The sepia-toned photograph shows an earnest-looking young Second Dragoon Guard mounted on a horse during the First World War. As I look at the image, it takes me back to my childhood as the man in the photo is my grandfather. I can remember sitting on his lap in front of his large roll-top desk while he told me stories about horses. There was a sense of mystery when he put the key in the lock and the curved wooden slats that covered the front clattered back to reveal tiny drawers; it was like entering another world. Letters and papers nestled in pigeonholes, and bottles of ink and pots holding pens stood guarding the drawers that contained myriad fascinating items to my child's mind such as paper clips, rubber bands, pen nibs and drawing pins. Sometimes, if I was lucky, the drawers also held a sweet.

My grandfather would periodically pause from his story to open one of the tiny drawers. I was allowed to say which drawer could be opened—only one. Granddad made much theatrical drama of opening a drawer; he took the drawer and, after much ado, shaking its contents around while I waited, transfixed with excitement, he eventually showed me inside. I could look at the drawer's contents but not touch. If the drawer held a sweet, I was allowed to pick out the sweet. His stories also fired another passion that shaped my life—a love of horses. Often he told me about the horses he used to ride and look after during the war, and how each horse had a particular character—he knew them all. His favourite was Punch, and he explained how Punch used to like to be tickled just behind his ears. My grandfather's stories seemed to hold a profound power in kindling my imagination, particularly his tales about horses—they seemed to be animals that you could ride in everyday reality, but they were also magical creatures that could transport me to other places in my imagination, and this they would do when, years later, as an anthropologist studying magic, I came to have a spirit connection with a special horse. Although I did not know it at the time, horses have often been shamans' guardian spirits from Europe to Siberia, and the shamanic flight to other realms has been widely expressed as a horse's gallop.[17]

Over time, I slowly began to understand the role that my grandfather has played in my life. His storytelling at the magical desk had aroused my fascination with the timeless moment, a shift in consciousness which enabled a different way of seeing things and a lifelong love of horses—so much so that I felt that I had horses in my blood. Although I did not realize it at the time, this was an early training of my mind to find magic in everyday things; the combinations of everyday objects in the tiny wooden drawers created interesting patterns; they were like a kaleidoscope picture that formed and reformed in varying ways.

Years later, after I had done my anthropological training and during fieldwork with Jo Crow, the horse would reappear in my life. As soon as I started work, I managed, with a great deal of saving up and borrowing of money, to buy a horse of my own, and eventually, after some years, bred a foal from this horse, which I named Cielle. This foal, as she grew, taught me about the emotional involvement that underlies magical consciousness. Cielle was not courageous—when she was old enough to ride out, she was scared by all sorts of things. I used to say to her, 'Look at that dangerous butterfly in the hedge, Cielle!' as I was riding her, but the tone of my voice would calm her down. She trusted me, and this was shown clearly when her first foal was born. The foal would not get up, and Cielle, instinctively knowing something was wrong, was anxious for human assistance. The foal's fight for life was short-lived, and he died a couple of days later.

We tend to think that horses do not have the same feelings as humans, but Cielle's process of grieving for her foal was plain to see. It was this experience that would make a magical connection between the horse and me—she seemed to understand something profound about the experience of death. Many years later, it became necessary to put Cielle down due to severe colic and a suspected twisted gut. Cielle's death had a very great impact on me—I felt overwhelming sadness.

It was through Cielle's death that I really learnt about thinking with my heart. Magical thought is essentially emotional—it is built upon affective relationships developed over time. It was in the period directly after Cielle's death that my emotion about the horse increased through the grieving process. Jo Crow had invited me to join her rattle-making workshop at Ridge Farm in Sussex, and I readily accepted her invitation. Shamans use rattles to contact magical realms; I knew intuitively that the rattle I would make would be a horse rattle.

This was how I came to be lying on the floor journeying in an alternate state of consciousness to find the spirit of the rattle. Jo was drumming, and the drumbeats helped me to shift my awareness so that I entered a cave in my journey in my imagination.[18] I saw Cielle's colour—her bay coat gleaming. It felt as if Cielle's spirit went right through me, and as her spirit came out of me, I started riding her, and she became a snake-dragon, turning into snake vertebrae—she was the snake's vertebrae, white and glistening. We moved down and through, and around, spiralling downwards until she was me, and I was her. The journey was short but very powerful.

After the journey, all the participants of the workshop went out into the grounds of Ridge Farm to find significant parts for their rattles. I needed to find some stones or other materials to put inside to make the rattling sounds. As I walked out into the daylight along a small path, I felt myself drawn towards a small horse chestnut sapling. It felt right to take one of its five-fingered leaves to put inside the rattle. The horse chestnut was the connection in everyday reality with the spirit horse. Other things came to me, too.

Back inside the farmhouse, we constructed our rattles according to Jo's instructions. First, the design of the horse head had to be drawn on paper to make a template; then the template image was transposed onto rawhide and cut out. After a period of soaking, the leather became soft enough to sew around the edges. After being stuffed with sand to get the right shape, and drying overnight, the horse head was ready to be emptied of the sand and filled with objects such as small stones from the beach or seeds to make it rattle, before the handle was inserted. This was the stage when the rattle started to feel as though it were coming alive. I put the horse chestnut leaf inside, along with several other things that rattled, and bound the handle in place. I now had a working rattle to connect with Cielle in the spirit world; the process of making it had drawn me into a deeper emotional connection with the horse.

The following week, when I had returned home, it felt as if the rattle were telling me how it wanted to be decorated. Somewhat to my surprise, the horse's head became dark blue, and there were black and red dotted lines running through the blue. She had no eyes, but she was touched with gold: her bridle was bright royal blue and was adorned with gold and silver bells that tinkled at the slightest movement; red ribbons hung from her bridle. Where I had joined the wooden handle to the rattle was bound in soft chamois leather, and over the leather was stitched five gold and silver periwinkle shells; falcon and pigeon feathers were attached. I added some of Cielle's mane to the rattle. To me, Cielle had become a dragon-horse, a Blue-Black Nightmare. When I rattled her, the sound was like the sound of her hooves, and the bells tinkled.

The rattle was a symbol of my participation with a spirit realm—it linked my experiences with Cielle and created meaningful relationships in my mind. With the help of the rattle, I slowly realized that Cielle was a magical horse that could help me understand more about death. As a mare in this reality, she had lost her offspring, and this is the worst thing that can befall a mother—equine or human. As a magical horse, I felt that Cielle knew about death and that she would travel with me to find death as a deep place of mind. Cielle felt like a warm presence that would help me overcome my fear, as I had helped her overcome her fears when she was alive in everyday reality.

In my case, the early relationship with my grandfather and the snake-dragon journey in my imagination combined with making the rattle, and the connections involved, including the association with the horse chestnut tree, were a crucial part of the whole experience, through which I gained a deeper understanding of myself and of death.

The feeling of riding the snake-dragon was so intense that I felt my bodily boundaries merge with this other being—I became the horse-snake-dragon. Cielle had died, but her spirit was still alive, and her death had created a strong emotional connection between us.

## NOTES

1. Susan Greenwood, conclusion to *Magic, Witchcraft and the Otherworld* (Oxford: Berg, 2000), p. 211.

2. Jo Crow, personal communication, 8 October 2002.
3. Oliver Sacks's home page, http://www.oliversacks.com, accessed 14 March 2009.
4. Oliver Sacks, 'The Mind's Eye', in David Howes, ed., *Empire of the Senses: The Sensual Culture Reader* (Oxford: Berg, 2005), p. 29.
5. Sacks, 'The Mind's Eye', p. 29.
6. Sacks, 'The Mind's Eye', pp. 29–41.
7. Transcript of audiotaped conversation with Jo Crow, 29 January 2003.
8. Mircea Eliade, *The Myth of the Eternal Return: Cosmos and History* (London: Arkana, 1989), pp. 259–64.
9. Caroline Humphrey, with Urgunge Onon, *Shamans and Elders* (Oxford: Clarendon Press, 1996), p. 1.
10. Humphrey, *Shamans and Elders*, p. 362.
11. Humphrey, *Shamans and Elders*, p. 362.
12. This information was given on a U.K. Channel 4 television programme called *Mindshock: Transplanting Memories*, shown on 4 August 2007; see http://www.youtube.com/watch?v=sudmW97FZA0, accessed 26 March 2009.
13. Bronislaw Malinowski, 'Sorcery as Mimetic Representation', in Max Marwick, ed., *Witchcraft and Sorcery* (London: Penguin, 1982), p. 241; originally printed in Bronislaw Malinowski, *Magic, Science and Religion and Other Essays*, Robert Redfield, ed. (New York: Doubleday, 1954), pp. 70–84.
14. Bronislaw Malinowski, excerpt from 'Culture', in Edwin R. A. Seligman and Alvin Johnson, eds, *Encyclopedia of the Social Sciences* (New York: Macmillan, 1959), Vol. 4, pp. 634–42; reprinted as 'The Role of Magic and Religion', in William A. Lessa and Evon Z. Vogt, eds, *Reader in Comparative Religion: An Anthropological Approach*, 4th ed. (New York: Harper and Row, 1979), p. 41.
15. Malinowski, 'Sorcery as Mimetic Representation', p. 242.
16. Peter Pels, introduction to Birgit Meyer and Peter Pels, eds, *Magic and Modernity: Interfaces of Revelation and Concealment* (Stanford: Stanford University Press, 2003), p. 12.
17. Barbara Tedlock, *The Woman in the Shaman's Body: Reclaiming the Feminine in Religion and Medicine* (New York: Bantam, 2005), p. 35, quoting Paul Bahn and Jean Vertut, *Journey through the Ice Age* (Berkeley: University of California Press, 1997), p. 16.
18. This technique for altering consciousness has been made popular by anthropologist Michael Harner, *The Way of the Shaman* (New York: HarperCollins, 1990).

## FURTHER READING

Geurts, Kathryn Linn, 'Consciousness as "Feeling in the Body": A West African Theory of Embodiment, Emotion and the Making of Mind', in David Howes, ed., *Empire of the Senses: The Sensual Culture Reader*, Oxford: Berg, 2005, pp. 29–41.

Greenwood, Susan, 'Magical Consciousness', in *The Nature of Magic*, Oxford: Berg, 2005, pp. 89–118.

Hume, Lynne, *Portals: Opening Doorways to Other Realities Through the Senses*. Oxford: Berg, 2007.

Humphrey, Caroline, with Urgunge Onon, *Shamans and Elders*, Oxford: Clarendon Press, 1996.

Tedlock, Barbara, *The Woman in the Shaman's Body: Reclaiming the Feminine in Religion and Medicine*. New York: Bantam, 2005.

# 5 A MYTHOLOGICAL LANGUAGE OF MAGIC

A painting of the Golden Bough by eighteenth-century English Romantic artist Joseph Mallord William Turner captured James Frazer's imagination. The work of art depicted what Frazer called a 'scene of a strange and recurring tragedy'[1] in a sacred grove and sanctuary of the goddess Diana in Nemi, Italy. Frazer began *The Golden Bough*, his 1922 classic study in magic and religion, by describing the scene that Turner had painted. Frazer set about to explore Turner's dreamlike vision through mythology. Collecting facts and legends, Frazer found out that a certain tree grew in this sacred grove, around which 'at any time of the day, and probably far into the night, a grim figure of a priest, carrying a drawn sword and peering warily about him, might be seen to prowl'.[2] The dark figure was the King of the Wood,[3] a priest murderer searching for a man who had come to murder him and thereby claim the priesthood in his stead. A candidate for the priesthood could only succeed to office by slaying the priest, and having slain him, he retained office of the King of the Wood until he was himself slain by someone stronger or craftier.[4] Each priest guarded the tree, as the embodiment of Diana, with his life, probably worshipping it as his goddess and embracing it as his wife. The King served Diana, who was revered as the goddess of the woodlands and of wild creatures, and probably also of domestic cattle and of the fruits of the earth. Conceived as a huntress, Diana blessed men and women with offspring and granted women easy deliveries, according to votive offerings found at Nemi. Here, then, is a dynamic interplay of a relationship with nature that Frazer thought underscored all ritual.

Rites, such as those performed for Diana in her sacred sanctuary, were, for Frazer, 'the effects of similar causes on the human mind in different countries under different skies'.[5] Frazer thought that if he could show that such a custom had existed elsewhere, it might have existed universally.

Anthropologists have criticized Frazer's universalist search for a common, underlying meaning to myth, and also his butterfly-collecting approach to gathering data—his finding of many examples from around the world and putting them together out of context—but his work is important for an understanding of the associative thinking that so characterizes a magical mode of mind. This mythological pattern of the death and rebirth of kings of the wood reflects the decay and revival of vegetation: winter kills what has grown in spring, but life comes once more in a seasonal round. The gods of vegetation died violent deaths and were brought to life again,[6] and this cyclical representation of time, that might be expressed in a variety of different ways, is nonetheless typical of much magical thought. Frazer's use of myth provides a repository for understanding cosmological processes of mind. Behind the king of the wood/goddess Diana mythological events is a process of thinking that reflects a connection with the annual cycle of nature, and this can reveal much about the nature of the human psyche.

What is rather ironic about Frazer's study of mythology is that in the process of explaining myth, he demonstrates magical thought, but in the final instance, he denies the power of this thought. As we saw in Chapter 3, for Frazer, 'the fatal flaw of magic' lay in the mistaken applications of the association of ideas inherent in sympathetic magic. He noted that the principles of association were excellent in themselves and were 'absolutely essential to the working of the human mind', but legitimately applied, they yielded science, and illegitimately applied, they yielded magic, which he called the 'bastard sister of science'.[7] This view is historically inaccurate as magic contributed to the scientific enterprise; however, the view that magic and science are opposed categories of thinking has persisted in the social sciences, and nowhere is this more true than in the study of myth.

## MYTHOS AND LOGOS

Today, myth is often considered to be fictitious because it is associated with magic, but the early Greeks highly valued the poetic discourse of *mythos*. Speakers and storytellers could captivate and charm an audience by relating the fantastical adventures and misadventures of spirit beings that inhabited a different time and mode of living to ordinary people. 'While mythic narrative had its capacity to scandalize reason, it was also through the narration of these dramatic antics of the gods that fundamental truths of existence could be explored.'[8] It was only later that *mythos* became opposed to *logos*, and *logos* became privileged. *Logos* is Greek for 'word, speech, discourse', and also 'reason' and the use of rational and logical argument. As a word, *myth* only came into the English language during the nineteenth century, and at this time, it already had the negative connotations accorded to it from classical Greece, where it referred to a nonrational, or even deceptive, set of ideas or false consciousness,[9] as in my use of the term to explain why Lévy-Bruhl's ideas about native thought had been largely ignored by anthropologists in the introduction to this book. The opposition between *mythos* and *logos* occurred at the time when the written text gained prominence over oral poetry. There was a trend that accompanied a shift to democratizing speech: no longer was speech the preserve of the eloquent—all had the right to the rational language of *logos*: 'each man, through the faculty of reason, could fight on equal terms through discussion and counter-argument.'[10]

The purpose of *logos* was to establish truth on the basis of the so-called laws of thought and thus through logical, critical and detached intelligence alone. Everything earlier attributed to speech as the power to impress and convince was reduced to *mythos*, 'the stuff of the fabulous, the marvellous'.[11] Later Greek writers used myths to illustrate the superiority of *logos*. Plato, while being a supporter of *logos*, did not deny the potency of myths; indeed, he used them to elaborate his own philosophical theories,[12] as in his famous myth about the darkness of the cave with its sensory impressions that obscured the light of an eternal and unchanging realm of Ideas, a timeless and nonsensory reality, as we saw in Chapter 2. More recent writers have also used the methodology of *logos* to understand *mythos*. My aim in this chapter is to reevaluate myths not as a language of *logos*, but as a language of *mythos*. Before we can examine myths as a doorway into magical consciousness, we need to understand how *logos* has taken centre stage in one influential anthropological theory of mythology that seeks to understand the language of myths scientifically.

## The Language of *Logos*

Myth is a language that can provide insight and a novel perspective that takes us from our normal, everyday world into another place in the mind. Belgian-born anthropologist Claude Lévi-Strauss (1908–) realized this feature when he pointed out that myth did not provide a picture of ethnographic reality, but rather, was a way of reaching unconscious categories of the mind.[13] For Lévi-Strauss, myth had no location in chronological time, but it had a character that it shared with dreams and fairy tales—in myth, animals talk with humans and the extraordinary is a matter of course. Lévi-Strauss's project was to isolate myths from their social context—he wanted to demonstrate that myths emerge not from social action, but independently, from a mind that lies behind culture. He went on to analyze myths as a language of the unconscious. Thinking that Western brains were too contaminated by cultural training in a high-tech society, he looked at South American Indian and Australian Aborigine mythology. Lévi-Strauss's *Mythologiques* is an in-depth study of more than 800 American Indian myths, through which he sought to reveal universal mental structures.

Sigmund Freud (1856–1939), the Austrian founder of psychoanalysis, was a great influence on Lévi-Strauss. Thinking that the mind could not be equated with consciousness, Freud put the emphasis on the unconscious, which he saw as dark, aggressive and sexual. Freud was not the first thinker to formulate the unconscious,[14] but he tried to bring a study of the unconscious into the domain of scientific enquiry. Freud's views have been very influential in Western societies, and they are based upon a view that the unconscious is potentially dangerous; it must be firmly controlled by society. In Freud's view, the unconscious was not simply those ideas or motivations of which we are unaware, but rather, a dynamic conception of forbidden drives and desires, impulses and instinctive strivings. For Freud, the conscious mind was formed through its negation, prohibition, taboo and denial of the unconscious. The unconscious is rooted in repressed desires, and consciousness expends energy trying to stop and bar knowledge of these desires. In his 1923 work *The Ego and the Id*, Freud distinguished between a superego, which judged an ego, which in turn regulated an id, which was formed from the unconscious; these biologically given processes and impulses strove for consciousness.

Lévi-Strauss examined the process of the transformation of the underlying unconscious but logical structure of myths by searching for their complex symmetry on different levels. Elements of the myth (thesis) were broken down into pairs of contraries (antithesis) that were resolved through mediators (synthesis and thesis), which were further broken down into contraries (antithesis again), and so on. In the process, he hoped that the structure of the unconscious would be revealed. The function of mythology was to exhibit publicly (though in disguise) ordinary unconscious paradoxes. The hidden message was the resolution of unwelcome contradictions.

Myths, as understood by Lévi-Strauss, were the precursor of science: they show the basic structure of mind and the essential structural principles through which all cultural forms were expressed. However, Lévi-Strauss's huge corpus of work on myth subsumes *mythos* to *logos*—he reduced the meanings of myth to a study of the mind that thinks not magically or analogically, but logically. Lévi-Strauss saw religion as a domain of confusion and emotion, and science as a domain of distinction and reason.[15] Myths showed the essential structural principles that all cultural forms expressed—the basic structure of mind. Lévi-Strauss, in his attempt to show the distinctive features of native thought, elaborated some of the key features of what he saw as scientific thought, particularly the use of analogy (see Chapter 3) and what he termed *bricolage* (the idea of creating something from whatever was at hand), as central to scientific theory.[16]

Lévi-Strauss thought that 'the savage mind' proceeded through understanding with the aid of distinctions and oppositions, rather than affectivity, confusion and participation.[17] He thought that primitive thought was prior, untamed and wild. By contrast, modern thought was tamed and domesticated. Untamed thought was ordered but had no special tools—it fashioned things from whatever was available (bricolage)—whereas modern thought was very precise and specialized. His focus was on the study of cultural symbolism as a mode of thinking that was detached from individual experience and emotion. As myth was largely unconscious and analogous to language, it could be broken down into codes. All behaviour was a language—a vocabulary of grammar and order—not a fieldwork enterprise. Lévi-Strauss reduced hundreds of South American myths to a coding scheme by which one myth could be transformed into another, with the aim of allowing the organization of structures to reveal itself: the myths revealed their own logic.

As a structuralist, Lévi-Strauss thought that there was a single basic structure of binary thinking underlying all human mental functioning and behaviour. This structure could be discovered by linguistic analysis. Structural linguistics offered the hope of a bridge between the human and the natural sciences—it was a scientific approach to language popular in the 1940s and 1950s. Structural linguistics replaced the nineteenth-century referential theory of language, in which words as sound referred to objects in the material world—for example the sound we make when we say the word *bird* refers to a feathered creature that flies, nests and lays eggs. In structural linguistics, there is no connection between a sound and its referent word; this is because sound refers not to the material world, but to a *concept*, and this concept is only understood in its relationship to an internal system, not to anything external to it.

Drawing on de Saussure's *semiology*, the science of forms, Lévi-Strauss took the view that language was a set of signs. A sign consisted of a signifier (e.g. bird) and the signified (as concept of the bird). Both signifier and signified combined create a sign that was the total of the concept and the image of the bird that had meaning, for example a white dove is a sign (symbol) of peace and hope. Language was a system of signs and could be studied apart from society. Lévi-Strauss used semiology in his attempt to understand myths. Rather than looking for the individual meaning for a specific myth, he superimposed whole sets of myths to arrive at a pattern—a symbolic system of symbols. This symbolic system could have a variety of interpretations, and he tried to show how they were used by the human mind. For him, symbols and particular relations might differ from culture to culture, but there was universality in the way that the human mind addressed them. If it could be shown that all peoples everywhere thought articulately in the same way, that they had the same logic, then this logic would provide the common framework for an analysis of all cultures.[18] Lévi-Strauss reduced mythology to *logos*, an abstract and emotionless code of logic equivalent to causality, and *mythos* was subsumed to *logos*. For comparison, let us now turn to an examination of *mythos*, a language of magic.

## A Language of *Mythos*

If *logos* is based on the discovery of abstract and emotionless codes, *mythos*, by contrast, has the ability to involve its audience emotionally—working on both conscious and unconscious aspects of mind to bring about change in the listener, as explained by Leah, one of my informants mentioned in Chapter 2. Indeed, the Greeks considered the affective performative aspect of myth important to its power.[19] The performance of myth brings it alive in terms of the feeling of its messages through the body. In this section, I will use two examples from my fieldwork to show the effects of the experience of engaging directly with mythology—myths become embodied through feeling them. My first example is from my work among Western practitioners of magic and concerns a group of pagans seeking connection with an ancient theme in European folklore called the 'Wild Hunt'.

### A Wild Hunt Challenge

During my fieldwork, I found that myths have the ability to take us from the normal, everyday world into another place within the body—the narratives and stories of myths are *felt*. The psychologically powerful mythological theme of death, fertility and regeneration, as pointed out by Frazer, is powerful for many Westerners who want to get in touch with the rhythms of nature (see Chapter 5). This was clearly demonstrated to me while I was conducting fieldwork with pagans in East Anglia, England. I had been invited by a group of witches to undergo a confrontation with death in the form of spectral beings in a wood near Norwich at night. I had got to know a local pagan witchcraft group, and each year, they held a 'Wild Hunt Challenge' in a nearby wood. If an invited person successfully completed the Challenge, it was said that he earned the right of the cooperation of the spirits of the area.[20]

The mythology of the Wild Hunt is a framework for experiencing the natural cycle of life and death. The night flight has been an ancient theme in folk beliefs, and it involves an ecstatic journey made by the living into the realm of the dead. Many modern witches have incorporated this folklore into their present-day rites. According to Doreen Valiente (1922–1999), a well-known witch and one-time high priestess to Gerald Gardner, the founder of modern witchcraft, Herne, the leader of the Hunt (also known as the Horned God, the Oak King, and the Greenwood Lord), carries off the souls of the dead into the underworld and leads out the Hounds out on the chase at Candlemas. Gwyn ap Nudd and the Wild Hunt are also called upon to prowl beyond the witchcraft circle as a 'protective element keeping all that has no right to enter the circle away'.[21] Valiente, who lived in Sussex, England, notes how on Ditchling Beacon, the highest point on the Sussex Downs, an ancient earthwork is haunted by a 'phantom hunt, known locally as the Witch Hounds'. She says that 'listeners hear the cry of hounds, the hoofbeats of galloping horses, and the call of the hunting horn, but nothing is seen'.[22]

Richard and Louise, who were both in their early forties and ran a post office called 'Wizard's End' in a small Norfolk village, invited those interested to a Wild Hunt Challenge, to be held on 31 October at Samhain (Halloween), when it is said that the veil between this world and the other world is thin. The aim of the challenge was to gain mastery over an area of Gwyn ap Nudd's hunting ground. The plan was to walk the wood route during daylight to learn the way, and then repeat it at night in a timed challenge. If completed successfully, the challenged person earned the right of the cooperation of the spirit beings of the area, and to cut a staff from the wood. The emphasis was on competition, sport and mastery—a contest between the magician/ shaman and the land, with its elemental kings or nature spirits. This was a challenge shaped by the mythology and folklore associated with Gwyn ap Nudd. Richard, who said that he had been researching the folklore of the Wild Hunt on the Internet, explained to me that the Challenge was a 'guided meditation', in which the challenger tried to interact with the elementals of the wood to open up other ways of being and to learn how to use the senses:

> We are used by Herne and the Hunt to find things on this plane. It's like a territorial army exercise—learning to use them, to work with them, and them learning to trust us. It's a challenge.
>
> Normal people don't go into the wood at night. You take on the ambiance of the wood and learn. You come back charged. You survived! You learn. You hear different things, your senses go on overdrive and your ears are the size of elephants' ears. Last time I heard fairy bells. I strained to hear them and then I saw other people straining to hear . . . It was a lovely sound. Then there were fireflies . . .

Despite feeling some trepidation, I decided to do the Challenge when invited; I was determined to face my own fears about walking in the wood at night. The Wild Hunt Challenge opened up a different sort of understanding with nature through an initiation into the process of life and death—to be hunted, to be taken by the Hunt, is to face the dark, chthonic realms of the other world. The wild wood was the ideal place—it was dark, the realm of elemental spirits and a space apart. One could turn from the everyday world—the so-called normal—to put oneself into a position to be taken by the train of the ghostly dead. The mythology provided the context and the language for the experience.

In my case, I had to overcome my social conditioning that woods are indeed a dangerous place to be at night. They are full of the fearful creatures that lurk in the dark recesses of the subconscious. Only when I had decided that I was not going to allow myself to be frightened by my imagination did I relax and enjoy the elemental feel of the woods. The image of the soft greys and shadow, the damp smell of vegetation, the fine misty rain and the shapes and sounds of the trees and the rustling undergrowth is an enduring memory; it is one that gave me a very different understanding of nature and of my place within it—a wonderful experience. Through facing my fear of the dark wood, I could come to appreciate the beautiful and terrifying power of nature. I felt part of the rhythm of life and death. I felt as though

I had offered myself to the Wild Hunt as a sacrifice, and in turn, it had shown me the beauty of the life of the wood.

When I eventually arrived back in the car park, some people were still in the process of setting off on their challenge. As I walked into the circle around the fire, faces looked expectantly for my report on my experiences. As more came back, so the discussion and comparison of experiences grew. Richard said he felt a dark presence following him, which he thought was a large, black dog. Darren, who had arrived late and was wearing a black, army-style balaclava, saw a medieval knight sitting on a horse behind him to his right. He spoke to Richard about it afterwards and offered to take Richard back to the spot where he had seen it. Richard said that this was no good as it had been Darren's experience and that the knight would have vanished. Richard advised Darren to look at the armour in a history book to find out what the knight was. Richard spoke of the last Challenge and how, in a different wood, he had seen some Vikings. He had reached out to touch them, but they had backed off, making his hand and arm glow golden.

It was obvious that the experience of walking through the wood had had an effect on people that they could not immediately articulate. Ideologically, the Wild Hunt restores reciprocity between humans and nature; this reciprocity occurs through a 'strange and recurring tragedy' in the broad sense of the annual death of one aspect of nature so that life can continue, as Frazer noted. The Wild Hunt is the mythological pattern of associative thinking that connects with the process of nature. Such myths speak about magical consciousness as much as they speak through its processes.

## Odin Eats Freyja's Heart

My second example concerns a mythodrama enacted as a magical experiment to feel what a myth could mean on its deeper levels through the language of poetics and embodiment. Where Lévi-Strauss saw the levels of myth as displaying its underlying logical structure, I wanted to find out the deeper depths of aspects of the magical mind. Freud's pupil Carl Jung (1875–1961), the founder of the therapeutic practice of analytical psychology, developed an understanding of mythology more in tune with *mythos*. His interpretation of the unconscious was not as id, a repressed unconscious, but an aspect of the psyche struggling for expression.

During the period 1914–1918, Jung experienced a psychological breakdown, and for the rest of his life he sought creative explanations for, understanding the images and symbols that had arisen from his unconscious. Many elements of his theory stemmed from a powerful dream that he had had of a house. Interpreting the house as an image of his psyche, the upper storey was a kind of salon furnished with fine pieces in rococo style; the ground floor had medieval furnishings and a cellar. Descending from the cellar was a beautifully vaulted room that looked exceedingly ancient. Looking closely at the floor, Jung discovered a ring in a stone slab, which he pulled. The stone slab lifted, and he saw another stairway of narrow, stone steps leading down into the depths. 'I descended, and entered a low cave cut into the rock. Thick dust lay on the floor, and in the dust were scattered bones and broken pottery, like remains of a primitive culture. I discovered two human skulls, obviously very old and half disintegrated. Then I awoke.'[23]

Jung dreamt that his psyche was formed from different levels, leading downwards to a cave that represented the world of the primitive human within; an area that he thought was scarcely reached by consciousness. Jung viewed the psyche as divided into a personal unconscious, which consisted of all the 'forgotten material' from an individual's own past, and a collective unconscious, the inherited behavioural traces of the 'human spirit', as symbolized by gods, that led to access to wisdom and universal human experiences. Jung thought that people everywhere were predisposed to form what he called *archetypal images*—certain symbols found cross-culturally in mythology, fairy tales and religious symbols in the collective unconscious. The idea of the archetype was not new; Plato talked about archetypes as active, living dispositions, ideas that have general characteristics (see Chapter 2), but for Jung, these were not abstracted ideas that existed in some eternal transcendent realm, but rather, biological entities deep in the psyche.

To further explore what might be the deeper levels of the unconscious within this psychic space, I experimented with ritually acting out a story about the goddess Freyja and the god Odin. Together with Brian Bates, my psychologist colleague and magical partner from the University of Sussex, who had directed plays at the Royal Academy of Dramatic Art in London, I enacted a mythodrama based on a poem first written down in the Eddic *Völuspá*:

> I mind the folk war—the first in the world—
> when they pierced Gullveig with their pointed spears,
> and her they burnt in the High One's hall;
> she was three times burnt and three times born
> over and over she lives.
>
> Heidr men call me when their halls I visit,
> a far-seeing witch, wise in talismans, caster of spells,
> cunning in magic, to wicked women welcome always.[24]

The gods attack and three times burn a witch called 'Gullveig' in this poem. Most scholars consider that Gullveig and Freyja refer to the same person, and Hor is also seen by some to be another name for Odin,[25] a god with many aspects. This poem was written in northern Europe during the so-called Dark Ages, a time when people believed that the world was imbued with spirits and certain women were seeresses, specialists at prophecy. Named *völvas*, these seeresses sat on raised dais, with other women forming a circle around them, chanting, to draw in spirits to assist in the process of looking into the future.

The following fieldwork account, that comes from my imagination as I experienced the goddess Freyja, concerns what might have happened between Freyja, a member of the Vanir, a race of fertility gods, and Odin, who came from the Aesir, a race of warrior gods. Odin calls for a prophecy of his future, and Freyja enters Odin's hall as an ordinary seeress; at this point, he does not know her for who she is. Her divination challenges Odin's ideas about what his future might hold. I wrote this after my experience:

> *The falcon circled lazily on the thermals high in the sky. She let the currents of warm air carry her towards the sun, feeling the gentle resistance with each delicate turn of exquisite wing and tail feather. At any moment, she would dive down to earth, like a bolt from the blue, surprising her unsuspecting prey, but for the present, she was content just to enjoy the warmth of the evening glow. Below, the Seeress waited outside the hall. Wearing a black cloak with a strap studded with precious stones reaching to the hem, she melted into the growing darkness. Around her neck were three amber necklaces; she held white cat skin gloves, and on her feet were long, laced-up, calf leather boots. The warrior god Odin had summoned the Seeress. She could hear him and his men now inside the hall; there was laughter and shouting and general merriment, and tales were being told of victorious battles, each aspect dramatized and relived. The Seeress felt nervous as she ran her fingers down her staff; the smooth feel of the wood comforted her, reminding her of her magical connections. She knew she was in touch with her magical power—she felt it as she felt the blood coursing through her veins—but she also knew that she faced a challenge, for she was to conduct a divination for Odin. He had called her. Intuitively, she knew that this was going to have enormous repercussions, but having been asked, she had no will to resist; indeed, she could not resist, as it would be against the course of nature.*
>
> *It seemed that she had been waiting for eternity, but suddenly, the hall door was flung open. A figure strolled out into the darkening evening, and the gleam of the fire inside cast shadows onto the surrounding land. It was Odin himself. He was a handsome man, a successful warrior and a well-respected leader; he had a commanding presence quite separate from the impressive quality of his high-ranking attire. He approached the Seeress. She faced him, and immediately, there was a tingle of attraction between them; she was well versed in the ways of love, and he could sense it. The Seeress gathered herself together, calling on all her experience and the wisdom of her ancestors. She demanded payment of gold and hospitality*

appropriate for the task she was about to perform. Odin agreed to her demands and strode back into the hall to make the necessary arrangements.

When all was correctly set out ready for the Seeress, she was invited inside and courteously escorted to the table to feast on mead, honey, dates and also the heart of a wild boar. She partook of the hospitality offered, and the conversation was respectful and polite. Six magnificent gold rings were put before her, and she greedily placed them on her fingers, holding out her arm to admire their shine in the firelight. This Seeress loved gold; she lusted for it. A platform had been constructed with a high seat strewn with furs, on which she was to perform her divination, and when she had satisfied her longing for gold, she mounted it. She was an impressive presence; the room fell silent, waiting to see and hear what would come next.

As she climbed into the high seat, she started to slip into trance, and as she looked down at the small circle of women who had been gathered to sing her into the spirit world, and the assembled crowd of warriors below, she felt them drawing into her, Odin, in particular. She settled herself into the seat, feet planted firmly apart and staff before her; it supported her with its twisted shaft formed by the growth of honeysuckle in its formative years, the falcon feathers bound to its tip gently swaying. She leaned forward, the staff taking the weight. Going deeper into trance, she felt the energy inside her move up and down the staff; she was riding it. Her back tingled, and there was a buzzing in her ears. Her body became a channel as, rocking, she soared upwards in spirit to the sun; the falcon was still circling lazily in the sky. The warmth of the sun filled her being as she felt herself expanding outwards. She lost sense of herself into the greater cosmos. After a while, she drew the solar energy into the conduit formed through her spine and the staff, holding it together with the energy of the gathered crowd at her feet. Then, in spirit, she descended to the depths of the earth, deep, deep into the dark and down into a cave behind a well, a well of wisdom of the source of all being. This was the cave of the female ancestors—the matrix of being. A circle of shaggy brown bears greeted her spirit; they were sitting in the cave around a fire, and they held the collected wisdom on which she drew. This was ancient knowledge. The Seeress felt connected to her source. She opened her heart; she was ready to perform her work.

Coming back into the hall in connected trance, she focused on Odin. She could sense him for what he was: she could feel deep inside him with a knowing that came from another place. His face was eager, looking up at her; it had a boyish charm, and she was attracted to his innocence beneath the flashing armour of the successful and victorious warrior. Odin had hung on the Yggdrasil, the World Tree, for nine nights, starving and pierced by a spear that sacrificed himself to himself until the runes of wisdom were revealed to him as he stared into the abyss.

The Seeress could feel his magical power; he had undoubtedly explored realms inaccessible to other men, but she also knew that he had much to learn. And he had to learn from her; she was to be his teacher. It would come at a cost to her, but in the process, she would learn, too. She felt the soft leather pouch that was suspended from her belt; it held her rune stones. The runes were indicators of the cosmic powers as they had been revealed to Odin, and she knew that this was a language that he understood. Having important information to communicate to him, it was vital that they understood one another.

First, however, she had to prove herself; she had to show that she could indeed see the patterns of fate and predict the future. Telling the assembled company of the creation of the world, how the first humans came to be, and about Yggdrasil, the sacred, cosmic World Tree, she also told of the war between the Vanir and the Aesir, two races of gods. Still in trance, she answered Odin's questions from her heart. Yes, he had been victorious in battle, and yes, he was a fair and just leader. The past was glorious—he was very powerful, and he was intelligent and courageous in the manner in which he conducted his affairs. This was an affirmation of the present situation. The six golden rings glinted on the Seeress's fingers as she extolled Odin's virtues to the attentive gathering, but what about the future? Odin demanded to know. It was all very well telling people what they already knew, but was the future to be glorious, too? Would Odin continue to be successful in combat? The Seeress demanded more gold.

As soon as three more magnificent rings were placed in her palm, she felt a shiver run through her, and she was frightened. Seeing into the future, as predicted by the current threads of fate, she would have to tell the company about the dissolution of the world and the final battle of the gods. Feeling impending violence, she was vulnerable and exposed, sitting alone amidst this hall of warriors. Indeed, she knew that she had come to face the danger, but she was still scared, as the reality of the situation dawned upon her. She could not speak, but fumbled instead into her pouch of divinatory runes. Feeling the smooth stones, she felt comforted, as the silence in the hall intensified. Everyone was waiting to hear, expecting more glory. Slowly, she drew out the rune Haegl, and there was a shocked hush. Surely there must be some mistake? It indicated dissolution and chaos due to dark female powers—this was not the expected divination. It challenged Odin's power, and he was mortified, and then his shock turned to anger. How dare this impostor make such a pronouncement! She must be a witch!

'Seize her, kill her and burn her!' he cried. His men dragged the Seeress from her commanding position and flung her into the fire pit that ran along the centre of the hall. They plunged their spears into her until she moved no more; stabbed and burning, her body lay dead. Odin began to calm down. How dare this woman make such proclamations; she must indeed be a witch, and good riddance to her!

*Challenging his power! The gathering broke up into small groups, discussing the evening's events, until a sound and movement attracted their attention. The be-draggled, ash-smeared and magnificent Seeress arose from the fire pit. She stood up and faced Odin, her eyes flashing defiantly. 'How dare you kill me!' she exclaimed. Odin was shocked. Perhaps his men hadn't finished her off properly. He ordered them to tie her up and repeat the process, silencing the niggling doubts in his mind that she was no ordinary witch. For a second time, the Seeress was thrown into the fire pit and stabbed, Odin adding his weight to the attack until it was made certain that she was indeed dead. The men retired, rather disturbed by the evening's events. As they were drifting off to sleep, another sound was heard from the direction of the fire pit. It was the Seeress stirring again. The men raised their heads in disbelief; surely it could not be the witch again. She had been killed! Maybe she wasn't a witch, and if she wasn't, it didn't seem right to kill a seeress with such magical powers. What other possible explanation could there be for her defying death in this way? This was a serious and bad omen.*

*The Seeress had indeed come back to life; she stood up again and once more faced Odin, soot stained, dishevelled, and covered in blood. She was calm and resolute as she told him that he had to take seriously what she had said about chaos and dissolution; this was to be his teaching. Odin had to enter the dark female do-main, and Freyja's power was there for all to see. Fear gripped Odin. He panicked and seized her himself, bound her tightly, beat her with her own staff and then plunged his dagger deep into her heart. This time, she fell and did not rise.*

*Freyja felt the rope being tied around her, the cords biting deep into her arms and legs. The pain numbed her mind as she was tightly bound; all that she was was being killed. Each strike of her magical staff reverberated through her—her own magic used against her! She knew that she could not survive. This was indeed the moment of her death, but she also knew that this was necessary for change to occur—it would alter the patterns of the cosmos. Having been contained, con-trolled and restricted in this way, she knew that she had to enter into the process willingly and with humility. Her last breath passed from her body.*

### Silence

*Seeing what he had done, and knowing that this time, she was really dead, Odin was filled with remorse, for it was at this moment that he realized that this was no ordinary seeress; this was indeed the goddess Freyja. A god cannot kill a god-dess! Ordering his men out of the hall, he paced around, unsure of what to do. None of his skills in fighting and battle had prepared him for this. He looked down on Freyja's burnt and bloody body, lying on the earth floor of the hall, and suddenly, he was filled with love for her. His heart opened, and he began to see in a different way. Intuitively, Odin reached for Freyja's blackened and charred heart and, kissing it, put it into his mouth to eat.*

*The wind was roaring outside the hall, and the rain was pouring down; the trees were waving in the gale outside. The goddess Freyja started to feel the energy moving through her. It wasn't fierce, but gentle, and the wind seemed to be calling her. It took her to a beach, and she remembered the golden rings that Odin had given her; she saw them beneath the rippling waves of the sea, and the sea melted into her. She saw the sun reflected in the water, and the rings sparkled in golden rays; the sea beckoned her deeper into its greenish blue, shimmering depths. Freyja felt the primal power of the water and her connection with the deep well of wisdom outside the cave of the ancestresses. Then she felt again the power of the wind, and she knew it was the spirit of Odin. The wind howled as it raced through the treetops, as Odin came whistling through every fibre of her being and they descended together into the dark of the cave under the sea.*

***

This mythodrama can be interpreted in many ways—there are many explanatory levels—but I will show how it illuminates magical consciousness on three major counts:

1. The fieldwork account was written from my experience of embodying the goddess Freyja. The invocation of deities is a process by which a god, or some other form of spirit being, incarnates in human form.[26] The doctrine that a god can be incarnated in human form, as avatar (a manifestation or embodiment of this deity or released soul in bodily form), is common to Hinduism, Mahayana Buddhism, Christianity and the Sufis,[27] and it is also common to modern Western witchcraft. In my first ethnography, *Magic, Witchcraft and the Otherworld*, I wrote about Michelle, a music student and singer in her mid twenties, who was training to become a witch. She described how she felt when her initiator invoked a goddess of the moon down into her during a Drawing Down the Moon ritual:

> I have been aware of varying and differing sensations—these sometimes are quite personally significant, at other times less so felt, but always connected with or to some kind of transformation. A warm, tingling feeling, especially in my arms, is typically experienced—also, a change of voice as regards both pitch and tone, it becoming somewhat deeper and richer—a sense of something greater . . . always . . .
>
> . . . To me it is as if each time I do Drawing Down the Moon, I draw down another aspect of myself, another possible potential hidden within the psyche, within the soul—a power I believe we all possess but have forgotten how, or are frightened to fully access and make manifest in the world.

Michelle said that this rite brings out different and hidden potential within her, and I concur with this. When I invoked Freyja during the mythodrama, I experienced what I have recorded previously as Freyja, and this gave me a deeper understanding of the goddess and also of the magical participatory aspect of mind that flows through associations and connections to do with the symbols of the falcon, sun and cats, all associated with the goddess and all leading, in turn, to other associations.

2. In essence, this story is about the initiation of the god Odin by the goddess Freyja into a magical mode of mind. Freyja, as a ritual sacrifice, dies to be reborn and, in the process, initiates Odin into an ancient life and death pattern. In this sense, Freyja—like other mythological figures, such as the King of the Wood and Odin himself, who hung on Yggdrasil, the World Tree, to receive the wisdom of the runes—is a sacrificial saviour deity. Saviour deities, according to Frazer, originated in prehistoric vegetation gods, whose ritualized annual death and resurrection in the spring ensured the fertility of the fields and flocks. From earliest times, fertility deities have promoted human, animal and plant fecundity. Fertility is linked with death as well as life. Life necessarily feeds on death—animals are hunted and killed; the living must feed off the dead. Death is imaginatively transformed into life: the sun dies daily and is reborn in the morning, the moon dies monthly and the crops go through an annual cycle from sowing to harvesting—the life cycle continues. What dies in one form is reborn in another in this mythological pattern of life, death and rebirth.

3. The mythodrama expresses a change in consciousness. Why did the gods burn the witch? Odin, the successful and powerful warrior god, orders the attack on Freyja—she must be a witch, rather than a seeress. Freyja is stabbed three times and manages to rise twice, but the final assault kills her. However, she is brought back to life through Odin's remorse at what he had done. Through this act of violence, Odin is forced to confront his emotions, and it is this that teaches him to feel through his heart. It is the realization that he has killed Freyja that initiates Odin into thinking in this natural rhythm; he feels with his heart, rather than his head, the heart being seen as the centre of intelligence and consciousness, as discussed in Chapter 4.[28] Symbolically, Odin gave Freyja a boar's heart to eat. The boar was a sacred animal in early Germanic and Scandinavian countries, the emblem of the Vanir deities,[29] and Freyja had a sow aspect as a death goddess[30]; indeed, among her names, as given by the thirteenth-century writer Snorri Sturluson, was Sýr, meaning 'sow'. Boar symbolism has been found on Anglo-Saxon funeral pottery, and the idea of an otherworldly feast with the ancestors in another realm has left many traces in later literature.[31] Death is associated with sexuality in the ancient world view that links life and death. Odin eating Freyja's heart is a sexual metaphor: eating equals sex between Vanir and Aesir; it also unites the elements of air and water, and water and fire (the latter two combinations being elemental attributes of Odin and Freyja, respectively).

In this context, the sexual eating should not be taken as an act of violence; instead, it represents a relationship of reciprocity between different elements. There is participation (interdependence) between humans and the rest of nature.

It can be argued that myths are so rich and complex that they can be used to express many things, from the logical code that underpins human rational thought, as claimed by Lévi-Strauss and the language of *logos*, to the more holistic awareness of *mythos*. In essence, myths hold the possibility of both these interpretations, and many more besides, as we shall see in the final chapter of this book.

## NOTES

1. James Frazer, *The Golden Bough: A Study in Magic and Religion* (Ware: Wordsworth, 1993), p. 1.
2. Frazer, *Golden Bough*, p. 2.
3. Pointing out that historically, kings have been revered not merely as priests, but as intercessors between man and god, Frazer, in the *Golden Bough*, described how they were able to bestow upon their subjects blessings that went beyond the reach of ordinary mortals. Kings were expected to give rain and sunshine and to make the crops grow. This was a part of an early mode of thought in which there was no distinction between natural and supernatural elements; the world was pervaded by spiritual forces. In early societies, the king was frequently a magician as well as a priest—he needed to understand magic (pp. 1–11). There was a widespread practice of dismembering the body of a king or magician and burying the pieces in different parts of the country to ensure the fertility of the ground and fecundity of man and beast (p. 379).
4. Frazer, *Golden Bough*, p. 1.
5. Frazer, *Golden Bough*, p. 386.
6. Frazer, *Golden Bough*, p. 362, finds comparative examples in the ancient Egyptian god Osiris, whose death and resurrection were annually celebrated through corn rituals. But, Frazer argues, Osiris was more than a spirit of the corn; he was also a tree spirit, and this might have been his original character (p. 380).
7. Frazer, *Golden Bough*, pp. 49–50.
8. Nigel Rapport and Joanna Overing, *Social and Cultural Anthropology: The Key Concepts* (London: Routledge, 2000), p. 271, citing J. P. Vernant, *Myth and Society in Ancient Greece* (New York: Zone Books), pp. 206–7, 220; originally published as *Mythe et société en Grèce ancienne* (Paris: Librarie François Maspero, 1974).
9. Rapport and Overing, *Social and Cultural Anthropology*, p. 272.
10. Rapport and Overing, *Social and Cultural Anthropology*, p. 271.
11. Rapport and Overing, *Social and Cultural Anthropology*, p. 271, citing Vernant, *Myth and Society*, pp. 207–8.
12. Rapport and Overing, *Social and Cultural Anthropology*, p. 271.
13. Lévi-Strauss's main works, apart from his autobiography *Tristes Tropiques* (Paris: Plon, 1955), are 'The Elementary Structures of Kinship' (PhD thesis, Univ. Paris-Sorbonne, 1947); *Totemism*, trans. R. Needham (Boston: Beacon, 1963); *The Savage Mind* (London: Weidenfeld and Nicolson, 1968), also published as *La Pénsee Sauvage* (Paris: Librairie Plon, 1962), on classificatory systems of the human mind; *Mythologiques: The Raw and the Cooked*, trans. John Weightman and Doreen Weightman (London: J. Cape, 1969); *From Honey to Ashes*, trans. John Weightman and Doreen Weightman (London: J. Cape, 1973); *The Origin of Table Manners*, trans. John Weightman and Doreen Weightman (London: J. Cape, 1978); and *The Naked Man*, trans. John Weightman and Doreen Weightman (Chicago: University of Chicago Press, 1981).

14. The seventeenth- and eighteenth-century philosopher Leibniz viewed the unconscious as a dynamic principle underlying consciousness, and he influenced German philosophers Von Schelling, Hegel, Schopenhauer and Nietzsche.

15. Lévi-Strauss, *La Pénsee Sauvage*, pp. 295–302; cited in Robin Horton, 'Lévy-Bruhl, Durkheim and the Scientific Revolution', in Robin Horton and Ruth Finnegan, eds, *Modes of Thought* (London: Faber and Faber, 1973), p. 274.

16. Pierre Auger, 'The Regime of Castes in Populations of Ideas', *Diogenes*, 22 (1958); cited in Horton, 'Lévy-Bruhl, Durkheim and the Scientific Revolution', p. 280.

17. Lévi-Strauss, *Savage Mind*, p. 268.

18. See Claude Lévi-Strauss, 'The Story of Asdiwal', in *Structural Anthropology* (New York: Basic Books, 1976), pp. 2.146–97; also printed in Edmund Leach, ed., *The Structural Study of Myth and Totemism* (London: Routledge, 2004), pp. 1–48.

19. Rapport and Overing, *Social and Cultural Anthropology*, p. 270.

20. For a fuller account of this Challenge, see Susan Greenwood, 'The Wild Hunt: A Mythological Language of Magic', in *The Nature of Magic* (Oxford: Berg, 2005), pp. 119–42; reprinted in James R. Lewis and Murphy Pizza, eds, *Handbook of Contemporary Paganism* (Leiden: Brill, 2009), pp. 195–222.

21. Doreen Valiente and Evan John Jones, *Witchcraft: A Tradition Renewed* (Custer: Phoenix, 1990), pp. 59, 154.

22. Doreen Valiente, *Where Witchcraft Lives* (London: Aquarian, 1962), p. 55.

23. Carl Jung, *Memories, Dreams and Reflections* (London: Routledge and Kegan Paul, 1963), p. 155.

24. This quote is from the *Elder Edda*, Paul P. Taylor and W. H. Auden, trans (London: Faber and Faber, 1973), p. 245, a collection of poems passed on orally and written down in the tenth century; cited in Brian Bates, *The Wisdom of the Wyrd: Teachings for Today from Our Ancient Past* (London: Rider, 1996), p. 171.

25. *The Poetic Edda*, i: *Lays of the Gods*, http://www.sacred-texts.com/neu/poe/poe03.htm, accessed 15 July 2009; Hor is also a name for a dwarf, according to the *Prose Edda*, written by Snorri Sturluson in the thirteenth century. It could be speculated that Hor was an elemental spirit of Odin.

26. See Susan Greenwood, *Magic, Witchcraft and the Otherworld* (Oxford: Berg, 2000), pp. 95–102, and also Greenwood, *Nature of Magic*, pp. 93–8.

27. Aldous Huxley, *The Perennial Philosophy* (London: Flamingo, 1994), p. 59.

28. Bill Griffiths, *Aspects of Anglo Saxon Magic* (Hockwold-cum-Wilton: Anglo-Saxon Books, 1996), p. 87.

29. Hilda Ellis Davidson, *The Lost Beliefs of Northern Europe* (London: Routledge, 1993), p. 111.

30. Barbara Walker, *The Women's Book of Myths and Secrets* (San Francisco: Harper and Row, 1983), p. 956.

31. Davidson, *Lost Beliefs*, p. 134.

## FURTHER READING

Bates, Brian, 'Heart of the Wolf: Transcending Warriorhood', in *The Wisdom of the Wyrd: Teachings for Today from Our Ancient Past*, London: Rider, 1996, pp. 168–91, esp. pp. 171–85.

Greenwood, Susan, *The Nature of Magic*, Chapter 6. The Wild Hunt: A Mythological Language of Magic, Oxford: Berg, 2005 pp. 119–142; reprinted in *Handbook of Contemporary Paganism*, James R. Lewis and Murphy Pizza (eds), Leiden Brill, 2009, 195–222.

Stevens, Anthony, 'Metapsychology: Jung's Model of the Psyche', in *On Jung*, London: Penguin, 1990, pp. 27–53.

# SECTION THREE
# PRACTICAL MAGIC

A witch performs no rite, utters no spell, and possesses no medicines. An act of witchcraft is a psychic act.[1]

—Edward Evans-Pritchard

Diviners are experts who embrace the notion of moving from a boundless to a bounded realm of existence in their practice. They excel in insight, imagination, fluency in language, and knowledge of cultural traditions and human psychology.[2]

—Barbara Tedlock

The palm of my hand . . . heals. But it doesn't work just anytime: only when I summon power. If there are people who are sick somewhere, my hands find them. Whenever someone thinks toward me, there on the tip of my middle finger it acts as if shot. If you touch electricity, you'll know what it's like.[3]

—Essie Parrish

Magic is often said to be about the purported art of influencing the course of events through occult means; it is a practice that is said can bring about certain effects such as causing harm or healing. It can be conscious or unconscious as well as rational and mystical, but above all, magic involves an immaterial psychic dimension to everyday reality; this is widely described as spirit. In this section, we will explore everyday magic, from the classic ethnographic work of Evans-Pritchard on Azande witchcraft, magic and oracles (Chapter 6) to divination and healing in various cultural settings (Chapter 7).

# 6   WEBS OF BELIEFS

After sitting in his hut writing notes around midnight, Evans-Pritchard decided to go for his usual nocturnal stroll before bed. Walking around the back of his hut amongst banana trees, he saw witchcraft in the shape of a bright light passing towards the homestead of a man called Tupoi. Evans-Pritchard followed the light, until his view was obscured and he did not see it again. He knew that only one member of his household had a lamp that might have given off so bright a light, but next morning, the owner of the lamp told him that he had not been out late at night, nor had he used the lamp. On making enquiries about the light, Evans-Pritchard was told that what he had seen was witchcraft. Shortly after, an old relative of Tupoi who lived at his homestead died. He thought that the coincidence of the direction of light and the subsequent death accorded well with Azande beliefs about witchcraft.[4] He said that he never discovered the real origin of the light that he saw at the back of his hut—it was possibly a handful of grass lit by someone on the way to defecate—but he could see how magical beliefs could shape social life. Indeed, Evans-Pritchard conducted his own life by following the advice of oracles and found it to be a satisfactory way of running his home and affairs,[5] as he recorded in his classic ethnography *Witchcraft, Oracles and Magic among the Azande*, first published in 1937, a few years after his exchange of ideas with Lévy-Bruhl.

Evans-Pritchard's ethnography is a landmark study that shows the rationale of patterns of beliefs about how about witchcraft is a reasonable way of thinking and ordering society—that Azande beliefs in witchcraft were illusory, but that the reasoning deployed on the basis of their mistaken premise was thoroughly logical—but this position is accomplished at the expense of an understanding of magical processes of mind. Evans-Pritchard examined magical beliefs from the point of view of the participants in a given social situation,[6] but as a Westerner well versed in scientific thinking, he did not believe in the reality of witchcraft *per se*. Evans-Pritchard's fieldwork on the Azande was conducted in the 1920s, and it records a society that was undergoing rapid transformation at the time and has long since vanished.[7] However, his work shows how magic can shape people's lives, and it is important for its sympathetic portrayal of what seemed like a radically different African culture to Westerners: it showed that Azande magic was not a passive object for the demonstration of alien and irrational beliefs, but rather, a source of knowledge that opened up horizons of understanding about the nature of human experience.[8]

At the time Evans-Pritchard was writing, it was commonly held among Europeans that so-called primitive people were irrational, backward, superstitious and intellectually inferior to civilized Westerners. Grand evolutionary theories were popular, which suggested that all societies had an inbuilt *telos* (an ultimate object or aim) that allowed them to evolve along a linear path from primitive to modern; in this scheme of things, witchcraft in Africa was evidence of a primitive type of thinking that had been outgrown by Europeans in a previous stage of development.[9] In addition, Evans-Pritchard's audience was composed not only of other anthropologists, but also missionaries and colonial administrators, as the Azande were under colonial rule.[10] It is thus not surprising that in his correspondence with Lévy-Bruhl on mystical mentality, Evans-Pritchard was keen to show that native ideas about magic were not irrational, but rational; but if Lévy-Bruhl had made natives more mystical than they really were, then Evans-Pritchard made them more rational than they really were. In so doing, he went to the opposite extreme to Lévy-Bruhl and rendered the mystical elements of magic less visible.

In making the case for the rationality of magical thinking, Evans-Pritchard took the Western scientific perspective that whatever was not perceptible to the senses did not exist.[11] In adopting this position, Evans-Pritchard left unexamined his own society's premises; these are increasingly seen as a product of a particular phase in the socioeconomic history of Western civilization.[12] In terms of our study of magic, he left magical consciousness (mystical mentality) largely unexamined, and so the total picture that Evans-Pritchard paints is ultimately skewed in favour of a rationality debate. Notwithstanding, Evans-Pritchard's ethnography of the Azande does illuminate some important aspects of magic, and these are as follows:

1. Magic can be seen as three sides to a triangle in a whole web of beliefs and behaviour; it does not compose isolated facts.
2. Magic is a social phenomenon that explains unfortunate events.
3. Witchcraft is an innate psychic act.

## Three Sides to a Triangle

It was Lévy-Bruhl, as Evans-Pritchard noted, who emphasized the view that ideas about magic were meaningful when seen as parts of patterns of ideas and behaviour. Each part became intelligible when it was seen in relationship to other parts, rather than as isolated facts. The issue for Evans-Pritchard was not the native ability or inability to reason, but rather, an understanding of the categories in which the reasoning occurred. What might seem to Westerners to be bizarre ideas about magic make sense when seen as part of a whole worldview.

So Evans-Pritchard demonstrated how magic, witchcraft and oracles formed three sides to a triangle of a rational framework of beliefs and knowledge for the Azande. The Azande used magic to combat witchcraft, and according to Evans-Pritchard, neither witchcraft, nor oracles or magic, could be seen in isolation; magic was an important variable in what he described as a ritual complex of witchcraft, oracles and magic[13]:

---

### Witchcraft (Mangu)[14]

- A material witchcraft-substance in the bodies of certain persons that could be discovered by autopsy in the dead and diagnosed by oracles in the living
- A supposed psychic emanation from witchcraft-substance which was believed to cause injury to health and property
- A substance of witch-doctors, 'witchcraft-phlegm', was produced by medicines to combat witchcraft[15]

---

### Oracles (Soroka)[16]

- *Benge*, the poison oracle that operated through the administration of strychnine to fowls (formerly, this was done to human beings)
- *Iwa,* the rubbing board oracle
- *Dakpa*, the termite oracle that operated by the insertion of the branches of two trees into runs of certain species of termites
- *Mapinko*, the three sticks oracle, operating by means of a pile of three small sticks[17]

---

### Magic (Ngua)[18]

- A technique supposed to achieve its purpose by use of medicines, usually incorporated into a magical rite accompanied by spells
- A 'special department of magic', leechcraft, that treated pathological conditions by empirical or magical means through physic (administration of drugs) or surgical (manual) treatment
- Also practised in associations, through communal magical rites open only to members

---

Evans-Pritchard thought that magic, as part of a complex of beliefs, operated in a social manner. Oracles were used for important social activities and also for every step of individuals' lives. Although some people were more keenly aware than others, everyone was involved due to the fact that the Azande legal system was based on the poison oracle. Issues of witchcraft were settled entirely through oracles; there was no possibility of discovering mystical action except through oracles. The Azande thought that the oracle spoke through fowls: a chicken remained under the influence of the poison for a long time before it recovered or died so that the oracle had time to hear all the relevant details concerning the problem placed before it and to give a well-considered judgement.[19]

Oracles and magic (see below) were two different ways of combating witchcraft. Oracles determined who had injured, or who was about to injure, another by witchcraft and whether witchcraft loomed ahead. Where witchcraft lay in the path of a project, it could be circumvented either by abandoning the project until more favourable conditions ensued or by discovering the witch with the ill will threatening the endeavour and persuading him to withdraw.[20]

'Oracles are a more satisfactory means of ascertaining the future, and hidden things of the present, than are witch-doctors,'[21] Evans-Pritchard claimed. As diviners, witch-doctors were not thought to provide more than preliminary evidence, which could then be placed before an oracle for corroboration.[22] In Azande life, the use of oracles was intimately bound up in social life. Divining through oracles was the province of men, a mechanism of male control and the expression of sexual antagonism, and this helped to shape Azande life.

Thus the association of these ideas created a mode of thought and behaviour that shaped Azande life.[23] The everyday thought of the Azande was dominated by a theory of misfortune caused by witchcraft. Their other anxieties were all ultimately translatable into a concern to work the oracles that would warn them of witchcraft and to obtain the magic to fend it off or punish it.

## Magic Explains Unfortunate Events

So magic should be understood in terms of the totality of the culture and society in which it is found; it must be seen as a 'relation of parts to one another within a coherent system, each making sense only in relation to the others, and the system itself making sense only in relation to other institutional systems, as part of a wider set of relations'.[24] What did Evans-Pritchard mean by this? Take the well-known example of the collapse of a granary. In Zandeland, sometimes termites eat the supports of an old granary, and it collapses. The cause of the collapse is well known, and even the hardest wood collapses eventually in the course of time. Evans-Pritchard explained how a granary is the summer house of an Azande homestead and that people sit beneath it in the heat of the day and chat or play the African hole-game or work at some craft. It might be, therefore, that people are sitting beneath the granary when it collapses, and they are injured. The issue is why these particular people have been sitting under this particular granary at the particular moment that it collapsed. That it should collapse due to termites is easily understood, but why should it have collapsed at the particular moment when these particular people were sitting beneath it?

Westerners would say that the granary collapsed because its supports were eaten away by termites—this is the cause that explains the collapse of the granary. They would also say that people were sitting under it at the time because it was hot during the day and it was a comfortable place to be—this is the cause of people being under the granary at the time it collapsed. To the Western mind, the only relationship between these two independently caused facts is coincidence: 'we have no explanation of why the two chains of causation intersected at a certain time and in a certain place, for there is no interdependence between them'[25]:

---

### Causal Explanation

1. Granary collapses due to action of termites
2. People sitting underneath during the heat of the day
   - Result is coincidence

---

Azande philosophy, on the other hand, can supply the magical link between these seemingly unconnected events. The Azande know that the termites undermined the supports of the granary, and they know that people were sitting beneath the granary to escape the heat and glare of the sun, but they also know that these two events occurred at a precisely similar moment in time and space due to the action of witchcraft—there is interconnection:

---

### Magical Explanation of Interconnection

Granary collapses due to action of termites: People sitting underneath during heat of the day: Collapse of granary on people at that time and at that place due to witchcraft

---

Witchcraft explains unfortunate events such as the collapse of the granary. Witchcraft combines with the use of oracles and magic into a pattern of thinking. This is what Evans-Pritchard referred to as a *web of belief*, in which 'every strand depends on every other strand' and the web is a 'texture of thought'[26], and we will explore this further below.

## Magic as an Innate Psychic Act

Witches, as the Azande conceive them, clearly cannot exist, says Evans-Pritchard. Witches are people who have a substance in their bodies that has been variously described as an oval blackish swelling or bag, in which various small objects, such as pumpkin and sesame seeds, are sometimes found and which is attached to the liver. Witches show no external signs of their condition, although people say that one can know a witch by her red eyes.[27] The anthropologist does not question the material explanation; other explanations—such as how the substances might have symbolic or spirit meaning as part of a mode of thought like magical consciousness—are not entertained. This is the major problem with Evans-Pritchard's ethnography.

The Azande believed that witches could shoot *ahu mangu*, things of witchcraft, into the bodies of those whom they wished to injure. This belief is not specific to Africa; for example, in the early Middle Ages in Europe, the same notion applied to elf shot, whereby little arrows sent through the air by elves were thought to cause harm.[28] In the case of someone being shot with *ahu mangu*, a witch-doctor, in his role of leech, would be summoned to extract the offending objects, which might be material objects or worms and grubs.[29] The Azande believed that some people were witches and could injure them by virtue of an inherent quality: 'a witch performs no rite, utters no spell, and possesses no medicines. An act of witchcraft is a psychic act.'[30]

Witchcraft was seen as an innate capacity to inflict occult harm, whereas sorcery was the deliberate act of achieving the same results through the use of certain medicines. Medicines could be used for various other good purposes, including to prevent rain from falling; to delay sunset; to ensure the fruitfulness of various food plants; to make a hunter invisible; to prevent wounded animals from escaping; to doctor spears; for women's fishing; for ironworking; for warfare (to doctor body and shield and to acquire enemy spears); to qualify as an operator of the rubbing board oracle; to produce true revelations in dreams; for sexual potency; to be in wealth, health and safety; to make babies grow strong; to procure abortion; to ensure that a new wife will settle happily in her husband's home; to avenge homicide, adultery and theft; for treating sickness and so on.[31]

# RECOGNIZING THE MAGICAL PATTERNS

Magic and witchcraft are not part of a clearly bounded and internally consistent form of knowledge but are a vital and continually expanding system of open horizons. Magic is dynamic and situationally adaptive; it refuses neat categorization. Magic presents new avenues of investigation and interpretation.[32] Evans-Pritchard's work on the magical beliefs of the Azande was groundbreaking in its time—it helped to change Western opinion on the supposedly irrational beliefs of others—but it also had limitations. Evans-Pritchard had argued against what he saw as Lévy-Bruhl's overemphasis on mystical participation; he wanted to show that Azande magic was rational, rather than mystical for the reasons already stated, but in the process, the essence of the magical experience became obscured.

For Evans-Pritchard, anything that could not be directly perceived by the senses could not exist. He did not experience magic: the role of the fieldworker was to be involved but not to cross the divide between objectivity (the scientific observer) and subjectivity (the affective experience). Unfortunately, Evans-Pritchard left it to his male servant Kamanga to experience the magic. In effect, what we have in this ethnography is a second-hand account of witch-doctor magic filtered through the Western understandings and assumptions of the anthropologist. This inevitably leaves the dimension of the experience of magic seriously lacking. While Evans-Pritchard's work is justly praised for its explication of the rationality of witch beliefs—thus removing the awkward division between so-called primitive and civilized societies—it does not do much to help us understand the actual magical processes involved in Azande witch beliefs. However, if we examine the beliefs of Azande witch-doctors, the specialist practitioners of magic as described by him, another participatory aspect of magical consciousness comes into view. It will be remembered that participation concerns a holistic orientation to the world that is both invisible and timeless, and it also involves a psychic connection in a pattern of relationships that connect spirit and everyday worlds.

Azande witch-doctors entered into a relationship with magic—they controlled witchcraft through 'good magic'. A witch-doctor was a diviner and a magician, a man or a woman[33] who used magic for good, socially approved purposes against witches. Instead of living in continual dread of witchcraft, they opposed it through the use of medicinal plants and oracles.[34] An initiate witch-doctor began to eat medicines to combat witchcraft with other witch doctors, sometimes from a very early age, but usually when the person reached the age of fifteen years or so. The medicines were seen to strengthen the soul and give the power of prophecy. The initiation process started with a public burial, and the initiate was given witchcraft-phlegm to swallow, before being taken to the source of a stream to be shown various herbs, shrubs and trees from which the medicines were derived.[35]

Evans-Pritchard employed his servant Kamanga to be initiated into the esoteric lore of witch doctors, and therefore his understanding is one distance removed. Nevertheless, we can still make out the participatory relationship between the witch-doctor, the Supreme Being, the ghosts and the medicinal plants. Evans-Pritchard described the search for plants made by Kamanga and his teacher, Badobo, by explaining that Zandeland was covered with a network of streams that flowed along either side of the Nile–Congo divide. Streams rise in springs that have eaten dark chasms out of the earth, which house snakes and are the homes of ghosts and of the Supreme Being.

There is a participatory connection in the minds of the witch-doctors between the fearful cavern, with its dark tunnels and underground trees; the ghosts; and the medicinal plants. The trainee witch-doctor has to learn to take the life of a medicinal plant in a certain manner so as not to upset the Supreme Being and the ghosts of medicine. If they crept along the ground on all fours, the ghosts would show them the plant for which they were looking.[36] Kamanga was instructed to give the ghosts of medicine a gift to ensure their cooperation; this gift established a connection with the spirits of the ghosts of the medicine plants. Payment for medicines formed a large part of the wider relationship of gift giving not only between witch-doctors and medicine plants, but also between teacher and pupil.

The initiate had to know about medicines to become physically and spiritually strong to resist the onslaught of witches; the same medicines were used to treat the sick. Often witch-doctors would make a magic stew from medicinal plants and eat it during a communal meal. A senior witch-doctor dug up a number of roots from the bush and prepared them before cooking. He placed them in a pot with some water, and he and his fellow witch-doctors watched them as they began to boil. Chatting and joking, they would talk about ordinary topics of conversation. After a while, when the water had become coloured from the roots, the pot was taken off the fire by the senior witch-doctor, who poured the liquid into a second pot, which was then placed on the fire for more boiling.

This procedure was accompanied by a few words asking for the welfare of witch-doctors as a whole and for the success of their professional interests. The roots were stored in a nearby hut for another occasion. At this point, says Evans-Pritchard, the witch-doctors focused their attention on the medicinal juices boiling on the fire—'this is the first sign in their behaviour that they are dealing with magical forces'[37]—and the following stages of cooking were accompanied by spells. It was important that the meaning of the spell was clear because the medicines had a commission to carry out, and they had to know exactly what that commission was; the medicines were not beseeched or entreated to act—they were told what to do, just as a boy would be told what to do when sent on an errand.[38]

The senior witch-doctor then prepared a ball of paste made from oil-bearing seeds ground down with a magic root into several small, round balls, one for each witch-doctor present. He placed the balls along the rim of the cooking pot, and first he, and then each witch-doctor, in order of seniority, flicked his ball into the pot. The senior witch-doctor then stirred the oil in the juices and addressed the medicines, partly on his own behalf and partly on behalf of the novice he was initiating. After addressing the medicines for himself—'May no evil fall upon me, but let me rest in peace. May I not die. May I acquire wealth through my professional skill. May no relative of mine die from ill-luck of my medicines; may my wife not die; my relatives are animals, my relative is eleusine, may my eleusine be fruitful.'—he addressed the medicines for his pupil: 'when you dance in the witch-doctors' dance may you not die. May your home be prosperous and may no witch-craft come to injure your friends . . . may none of your relatives die. Your relatives are animals, your father is an elephant, your father's elder brother is a red pig, your wives are cane-rats, your mother is a bush-buck, your maternal uncles are duikers, your grandfather is a rhinoceros.' The medicines are addressed further for the witch-doctor—'if witchcraft comes here to my home let it return whence it came. If a man makes sorcery against me let him die'—and for the pupil: 'let evil go over there, over there; let medicine make things prosperous for you. If anyone refuses payment for your services may he not recover from his sickness.' The medicine was further stirred and addressed by other witch-doctors. Eventually, the oil boiled to the edge of the pot, and the senior witch-doctor removed the pot from the fire and decanted it into a gourd before replacing the pot on the fire. The medicine was addressed further, and the witch-doctors made payment for their spells. The payments were placed in the sight of the medicines; this gave the magic its potency.[39]

The magical rite of gathering and preparing medicines focussed on the magical power of words: when the medicine plants were gathered by the witch-doctor, he called out, 'Spears! Spears! Spears! Spears!' and the medicines were prepared amid much addressing. As the medicine plants were collected, and as they were stirred by the witch-doctors, there was a corresponding expansion of meaning: the ghosts and the Supreme Being have to be approached correctly; the meaning of the spell, as the medicinal mixture in the pot boils, is made clear—it was told what to do—and other addresses are made for the safety, protection and prosperity of the magical workers, the initiate and their relatives. Magic is based on participation—the establishment of a connection through the gathering of plants and the ritualized addressing process of the preparation of medicine—thus establishing psychic and social relationships of magical associations.

## THE IMPACT OF WITCHCRAFT, ORACLES AND MAGIC

Evans-Pritchard's work has shown how magic is rational when understood within its own context, even though, in his view, it is ultimately inferior to science. Writing in the 1930s, he was very much a product of his time, as we all are. Ultimately, although Evans-Pritchard did much to render incomprehensible beliefs about magic comprehensible to Westerners, he did so without questioning his own assumptions about the nature of those beliefs. Or if we are to be generous, maybe he did question his assumptions, but the cultural climate in which he wrote only enabled him to go so far in expressing them, and they mostly remained private. Thus witches, as the Azande conceived them in this analysis, clearly could not exist. Witchcraft was a psychic emanation that was dealt with by magic, but because it did not fall into a category of understanding dictated by scientific reason, it remained largely unexamined.

For a decade between its publication in 1937 and the beginning of postwar research, *Witchcraft, Oracles and Magic among the Azande* had little influence, but in the next twenty years, it came to be used in crude functionalist ways that Evans-Pritchard could not have foreseen. Evans-Pritchard's interest seems to have been in showing how a metaphysical system could compel belief by a variety of self-validating procedures, but this approach was adapted to a more simplistic, functional hypothesis.[40] Evans-Pritchard's work showed how the Azande could tolerate discrepancies or contradictions in their beliefs, and that this could limit the kinds of questions that they asked. 'It might have been expected to stimulate more studies on the social restraints upon perception. Instead it fathered studies of micro-politics.'[41] Rather than appearing as infinitely complex, subtle and fluid, the relation between belief and society was presented as a controlled system with a negative feedback. Anthropologists strictly limited the questions they asked and restrained their natural curiosity. The assumptions of their model were no more critically examined than those underlying the Azande theory of witchcraft.[42]

It is clear that later work has not done justice to Evans-Pritchard's ethnography; it has been 'emasculated by being converted into a functionalist framework where it was interpreted as being about "social control"'—the sort of approach from which Evans-Pritchard continually distanced himself'.[43] The emphasis in most subsequent works has been on the social locus of accusations, theories of 'social strain',[44] and hypotheses concerning the dissolution of redundant relationships. This emphasis on the microsociological conception of anthropology has almost completely submerged Evans-Pritchard's most important ideas.[45]

Nevertheless Evans-Pritchard's work on the magical beliefs of the Azande had a wide impact, and it went way beyond the confines of academic anthropology, creating a bridge into history, philosophy and sociological studies. Being trained as a historian as well as an anthropologist, it was the wish of Evans-Pritchard to bring anthropologists and historians together, and he wrote the introduction to historian Alan Macfarlane's now classic 1970 work *Witchcraft in Tudor and Stuart England*. In this work, Macfarlane examined what ordinary people thought—so-called elementary village credulities—in contrast to the top-down approach of fellow historian Hugh Trevor-Roper. A value of Macfarlane's research was that he went beyond previous explanations of European witchcraft as no more than 'absurd superstition' to show that witchcraft beliefs formed an integrative system of thought and morals that had an important role in the social structure. Macfarlane, as a historian, could delve deeper than anthropologists into the history of witchcraft accusations as anthropologists were handicapped by the lack of social records. By contrast, historians could study witchcraft beliefs over a long period of time through written texts.

Unfortunately, Macfarlane's model suffered from the same functionalism as other studies of witchcraft of the time: in his account, accusations were an explanation for misfortune. There are movements among historians to move in new directions—in the areas of gender theory, the problem of attitudes to the body, notions of self and psychology—and to see the study of witchcraft as a cultural phenomenon and as a range of beliefs, as a language that allowed early modern individuals to 'pursue strategies, express emotions, define identities and negotiate fantasies . . . that offer present-day scholars major opportunities for gaining access to otherwise hidden social, cultural and imaginative worlds'.[46]

The exclusion of a sustained theoretical discussion of magic may reflect the overwhelming influence of rationalizing sociological theories. Evans-Pritchard took one important step in the development of anthropological approaches to magic, but ultimately, he was constrained by his time and his very theories of examination. We will return to this issue in the final chapter of this book. In the meantime, the next chapter shows some practical applications of the experience of magic in everyday life.

## NOTES

1. Edward Evans-Pritchard, *Witchcraft, Oracles and Magic among the Azande* (Oxford: Oxford University Press, 1985), p. 1.
2. Quoted in Barbara Tedlock, 'Toward a Theory of Divinatory Practice', *Anthropology of Consciousness*, 17 (2006), pp. 62–77.
3. Barbara Tedlock, *The Woman in the Shaman's Body: Reclaiming the Feminine in Religion and Medicine* (New York: Bantam, 2005), pp. 18–19.
4. Evans-Pritchard, *Witchcraft, Oracles and Magic*, p. 11.
5. Evans-Pritchard, *Witchcraft, Oracles and Magic*, p. 43.
6. Mary Douglas, 'Introduction: Thirty Years after *Witchcraft, Oracles and Magic*', in Mary Douglas, ed., *Witchcraft, Confessions and Accusations*, ASA Monograph 9 (London: Tavistock, 1970), pp. xiii–xvii.
7. The Azande, at the time they were studied by Evans-Pritchard, lived by soil cultivation, hunting, fishing and collecting wild produce. They grew eleusine, corn, sweet potatoes, manioc, groundnuts, bananas, a variety of legumes and oil-bearing plants. There was an abundance of game, and annual swarmings of termites were seen as a delicacy. They were smiths, potters, carvers and basket makers, but they had little opportunity to sell their labour or incentive to grow marketable produce, being largely shielded from outside influences, apart from government by the colonial administration. Eva Gillies, introduction to Evans-Pritchard, *Witchcraft, Oracles and Magic*, p. viii.
8. Bruce Kapferer, ed., *Beyond Rationalism: Rethinking Magic, Witchcraft and Sorcery* (Oxford: Berghahn Books, 2003), p. 4.
9. Henrietta Moore and Todd Sanders, eds, introduction to *Magical Interpretations, Material Realities: Modernity, Witchcraft and the Occult in Postcolonial Africa* (London: Routledge, 2001), pp. 2–6.
10. Peter Pels, Introduction to *Magic and Modernity: Interfaces of Revelation and Concealment* (Stanford: Stanford University Press, 2003), pp. 12–13.
11. Evans-Pritchard, *Witchcraft, Oracles and Magic*, p. 12.
12. Roy Willis, *Some Spirits Heal, Others Only Dance: A Journey into Human Selfhood in an African Village* (Oxford: Berg, 1999), p. 43.
13. Evans-Pritchard, *Witchcraft, Oracles and Magic*, p. 176.

14. Evans-Pritchard, *Witchcraft, Oracles and Magic*, p. 226.

15. The witchcraft generated by witch doctors was said to be quite a different substance to the witchcraft of witches, which was biologically inherited. There was a great deal of scepticism among the Azande about the degree of difference between the witchcraft of witch doctors and that of witches, and lay-people state plainly that it is ordinary witchcraft in their bellies that enables successful witch doctors to see it in the bellies of others; Evans-Pritchard, *Witchcraft, Oracles and Magic*, p. 113.

16. Evans-Pritchard, *Witchcraft, Oracles and Magic*, p. 228.

17. Evans-Pritchard, *Witchcraft, Oracles and Magic*, Chapters 7, 9 and 10.

18. Evans-Pritchard, *Witchcraft, Oracles and Magic*, p. 227.

19. Evans-Pritchard, *Witchcraft, Oracles and Magic*, pp. 124–9.

20. Evans-Pritchard, *Witchcraft, Oracles and Magic*, p. 176.

21. Evans-Pritchard, *Witchcraft, Oracles and Magic*, p. 120.

22. Evans-Pritchard, *Witchcraft, Oracles and Magic*, p. 120.

23. Evans-Pritchard, *Witchcraft, Oracles and Magic*, p. 33.

24. Edward Evans-Pritchard, *Theories of Primitive Religion* (Oxford: Clarendon Press, 1990), p. 112.

25. Evans-Pritchard, *Witchcraft, Oracles and Magic*, pp. 22–3.

26. Evans-Pritchard, *Witchcraft, Oracles and Magic*, p. 109.

27. Evans-Pritchard, *Witchcraft, Oracles and Magic*, pp. 1–2.

28. Valerie I. J. Flint, *The Rise of Magic in Early Medieval Europe* (Oxford: Clarendon Press, 1991), p. 115.

29. Evans-Pritchard, *Witchcraft, Oracles and Magic*, p. 38.

30. Evans-Pritchard, *Witchcraft, Oracles and Magic*, p. 1.

31. Both witches and sorcerers were social enemies, and both were classed together. Sorcery and witchcraft were opposed to, and were opposed by, good magic; Evans-Pritchard, *Witchcraft, Oracles and Magic*, pp. 176–9.

32. Kapferer, *Beyond Rationalism*, p. 7.

33. Evans-Pritchard, *Witchcraft, Oracles and Magic*, concentrates his attention on the training of male witch-doctors, only mentioning women in an aside about the appropriateness of behaviour in a divination dance: 'on those rare occasions when a woman witch-doctor takes part in a séance she keeps in the background and performs a sedate dance of her own. She does not attempt to imitate the violent dancing of the men, as this would be regarded as unseemly conduct' (p. 88). The anthropologist speaks about the difficulties of obtaining esoteric information about witch-doctors and employs his male servant to undergo initiation for the purposes of his research. A shortcoming of this research leaves the position of female witch-doctors largely invisible.

34. Evans-Pritchard, *Witchcraft, Oracles and Magic*, p. 65.

35. Witch-doctors were careful about magical plants, removing their stalks and leaves and hiding them lest anyone should seek to learn about their medicines by following them; Evans-Pritchard, *Witchcraft, Oracles and Magic*, p. 97. Power is built upon the witch-doctors' knowledge of such plants. The anthropologist could play off one witch-doctor against the other to get them to reveal their knowledge. As Evans-Prichard said, 'While Kamanga was slowly being initiated by one practitioner, it was possible for me to utilize his information to draw out of their shells rival practitioners by playing on their jealousy and vanity' (p. 68).

36. Evans-Pritchard, *Witchcraft, Oracles and Magic*, pp. 90–1, 99–101.

37. Evans-Pritchard, *Witchcraft, Oracles and Magic*, p. 92.

38. Evans-Pritchard, *Witchcraft, Oracles and Magic*, p. 177.

39. Evans-Pritchard, *Witchcraft, Oracles and Magic*, pp. 92–4.

40. Three main principles of the Azande analysis have been applied in later research: firstly, that witchcraft was seen as a 'lubricant', allowing grudges to be brought out into the open and providing a formula for action in misfortune; secondly, that accusations of witchcraft clustered in areas of

ambiguous social relations, where tensions between neighbouring rivals could not otherwise be resolved; and thirdly, that witch beliefs upheld the social system. See Douglas, 'Introduction'.

41. Douglas, 'Introduction', pp. xiii–xiv.
42. Douglas, 'Introduction'.
43. Malcolm Crick, 'Recasting Witchcraft', in Max Marwick, ed., *Witchcraft and Sorcery* (London: Penguin, 1982), p. 344.
44. See e.g. Max Marwick, 'Witchcraft as a Social Strain-Gauge', in Marwick, *Witchcraft and Sorcery*, pp. 300–13.
45. Crick, 'Recasting Witchcraft'.
46. Alison Rowlands, 'Telling Witchcraft Stories', *Gender and History*, 10 (1998), p. 301.

## FURTHER READING

Douglas, Mary, 'Introduction: Thirty Years after *Witchcraft, Oracles and Magic*', in Mary Douglas, ed., *Witchcraft, Confessions and Accusations*, ASA Monograph 9 (London: Tavistock, 1970), pp. xiii–xvii.

Evans-Pritchard, Edward, *Witchcraft, Oracles and Magic among the Azande*, Oxford: Oxford University Press, 1985.

Kapferer, Bruce, ed., *Beyond Rationalism: Rethinking Magic, Witchcraft and Sorcery*, Oxford: Berghahn Books, 2003.

# 7   MAGIC IN EVERYDAY LIFE

It was one rainy Hanover Day, a local Brighton street festival during mid July, when Jo Crow, the shaman introduced in Chapter 4, and I sat out on the street doing tarot readings for passers-by. The roads between the brightly coloured English Victorian terraced houses had been closed, and all manner of stalls had been set up, selling everything from home-made cakes and bric-a-brac to books and clothes. Local bands and musicians were playing, and the lamp posts were festooned with fluttering bunting. Our allocated spot was opposite the doors of the Church of the Annunciation, a building frequented by Aubrey Beardsley (1872–1898), the English art nouveau illustrator, author and caricaturist, who was born in Brighton. Earlier, the Hanover Day procession, composed of local children, government dignitaries and various bands, had emerged from the church and officially opened the day by parading through the streets. Jo and I had set up our stall to the accompaniment of the enthusiastic sound of hymns coming through the door. We sat out on the street at Jo's fold-up table, which was covered with a cloth and laid out with flyers advertising her services as a shamanic healer. Jo and I were going to do tarot card readings to help advertise Jo's healing practice.

Jo and I had got into the habit of doing tarot readings for ourselves, and for each other. The term *tarot* is a French adaptation of the Italian *tarocchi*[1] and refers to European cards probably derived from Islamic, Chinese, Korean or Indian playing cards used during the fourteenth century. Used in many different versions, these cards are now widely employed in Western magical traditions as a gateway into magical consciousness. Utilizing the cards to determine all manner of aspects of our lives, we had got into the habit of the regular consultation process, and I had begun to feel like Evans-Pritchard in relation to oracles—that this was a reasonable way to conduct my life. Even so, finding myself sitting in the road reading tarot was quite a strange experience for me; I felt very exposed as a worker of magic rather than an academic anthropologist.

We laid out two decks of tarot cards, the aim of which was to provide a point of interest—to draw people to the table. The tarot cards achieved the purpose, and after a short period walking up and down the street a few times, people started approaching us for readings. The day was wet, and between showers and the putting on and off of plastic sheeting, Jo and I attempted to deal with what ended up as a large queue of waiting people. The two ladies on the table next door looked on curiously as we started the readings. What surprised me was the urgency of the questions: 'should I stay in my present relationship or should I go travelling?' 'I want to know whether I should have another baby.' A couple needed to know whether to stay together. These were practical, intimate and personal questions—things that profoundly affected the askers. It felt as if Jo and I could not keep up with the demand; people wanted to know how to settle uncertainties.

In the middle of the street, between downpours of rain, Jo and I slipped into a magical mode of mind. It felt like we had opened up a participatory space between diviner and asker; we were bound within a wider pattern. We invited the person who asked the question to choose three cards, and then, as we looked at the cards that were placed face up on the table, we felt what came. The sense of what the cards meant did not come from a place of analytical thought, but from somewhere else. Whether this is called the unconscious or subconscious mind, empathy, feeling, emotion, interpersonal communication or intuition does not matter, but it does utilise magical consciousness.

Divination is an ancient and widespread means of seeking control or a way of exploring the nonmaterial world though unseen means; it is 'a way of exploring the unknown in order to elicit answers . . . to questions beyond the range of ordinary human understanding'.[2] During a divination, diviners utilize knowledge from oracular messages of various sorts, and 'to do so, they link diverse domains of representational information and symbolism with emotional and presentational experience'.[3] Having practical and spiritual applications, divination gives meaning in situations of uncertainty. Using a variety of methods, from gazing at a fingernail or at the moon to the Azande oracles described in the last chapter, divination can suggest answers to all manner of questions, from the ones that Jo and I were grappling with to the identity of a witch or a future marriage partner or the best time to plant crops.

One can imagine that our earliest ancestors needed information for their survival, on the movement and behaviour of animals for example. Much of this information would have come from direct observation, but also, trying to plan ahead to the future by other means would have been important. Contemporary Montagnais-Naskapi hunters, who live on the Labrador Peninsula, use animal bones and other objects for divination. The shoulder blade of the caribou is held to be especially truthful. The bone, cleaned, boiled and with a small handle attached, is held over hot coals for a short time. Cracks and burnt spots from the heat—representing a blank chart of the hunting territory—are read. The questions asked run along the lines of, 'What direction should hunters take in locating game?' The whole process involves dreaming, sweating and rattling. In divining with the burnt shoulder blade, the procedure is first to dream. This is induced by a sweat bath and by drumming or shaking a rattle. Then, when a dream of seeing or securing game comes to the hunter, the next thing to do is to find where to go and what circumstances will be encountered. Since the dream is vague and not localized, the hunter-dreamer cannot tell where his route will lie or specific landmarks he will see, and this is why he employs the shoulder blade. Drumming, singing, dreaming and divination by scapula combine as the modus operandi of the life-supporting hunt.[4]

All known peoples on earth have practised some form of divination. It has had a critical role in the classical world, in ancient Egypt and the Middle East and in the Americas, India, Tibet, Mongolia, Japan, China, Korea and Africa.[5] It is clear that throughout history, divination has been practised, as individuals grapple with the existential problems of everyday life. Divination was the most prized response to magical incantations, according to Apuleius (AD 124–170), a Roman philosopher who wrote *The Golden Ass*, a satire on the priesthood, and it was central to Greco-Roman and pre-Christian religion. In the *Timaeus*, Plato refers to 'daemones' as intermediaries between gods and men. Daemones were gifted with knowledge of the future and, in the pre-Christian world, were generally held to dwell in 'that murky layer of the middle air which reached from the moon to the earth'.[6] However, divination was a threat to the Church in early medieval Europe, and it was branded a sacrilegious pagan custom. The wise powers of angels were contrasted to the powers of demons by Augustine, who said that 'demons foretell many events that will come to pass. Yet, far above them is the loftiness of that prophecy which God brings to pass through the holy angels and prophets.'[7] Divination took many forms, from astrology, predictions from thunder and eclipses and the flight and cries of birds to the directions of sacrificial smoke. The early medieval Church attacked it wholesale.[8]

In Europe, people turned to cunning folk (usually rural-based practitioners of magic who employed herbalism, fortune-telling, astrology and charms to seek solutions to a client's problems) and astrologers (those who used lunar phases, planetary positions, eclipses and meteors as well as animal and plant behaviour; and others who drew up horoscopes to determine the position of the planets at the time of a person's birth) as people who used their occult powers to provide comfort and succour in the face of misfortunes, personal problems, vagaries, unfulfilled desires and the stress of life in an uncertain world.[9] Not just the province of ordinary people, all levels of society have been involved in matters of divination. As we have seen in the introduction to this book, in modern times, Ronald Reagan, President of the United States, was allegedly influenced by his wife, Nancy, who consulted astrologers about his presidential schedule,[10] and Princess Diana visited astrologers, too.

Divination can be explained solely as reflecting the unconscious mind of the person asking the question, the symbols of the tarot deck, for example, allow the unconscious to come to consciousness; it can release unconscious psychological issues and bring anxieties or problems out into the open for examination. However, there is also a spiritual dimension, viewed by many as providing a connection with the soul. In whichever way it is interpreted, divination offers a route into an understanding of magical consciousness.

## HEALING AS AN INTEGRATING FORCE

Another way of examining this magical mode of mind is through healing, an activity similar to divination in that it occurs cross-culturally and that it also releases unconscious feelings. More than just curing, more than just the application of a medicine, healing seeks to 'establish health and growth on physical, psychological, social, and spiritual levels; it involves work on the individual, the group, and the surrounding environment and cosmos'.[11] Weaving and mending the webs of communication, healing is a fundamental integrating and enhancing force that people experience through the trance state of magical consciousness.

How does magical healing work? It involves a knowledge of medicinal plant lore, but it also concerns the patient's faith in the healer and the healing process, which employs hope, suggestion, expectation and rituals that elicit what is known as the placebo effect. This works on the principle that if a person believes in the healing process, then the positive emotion that this engenders has an effect on the biochemistry of the body, with endorphins (neurotransmitters with pain-relieving properties thought to be connected with euphoric feelings generated in the brain), being released. The result is a reestablishment of emotional and spiritual equilibrium. In addition, songs, chants, prayers, spells and music produce emotional states that affect the way the immune system responds to the illness.[12]

Magical healing is different to the Western biomedical model in the manner in which it usually involves a spirit component. The dominant medical model is founded on the assumption that accurate knowledge can be gained from an impersonal assessment of sensory-based information that has been tested scientifically. It cannot effectively incorporate psychological, psychosocial or spirit factors[13]; the focus is on curing the disease through medical intervention, without consideration of spiritual aspects. By contrast, magical healing is based on a notion that spirit pervades all phenomena. Spirits are both the causes of misfortune and the means of its cure, and bad spirits have to be drawn out of a person. The role of the healer is to ensure that spirits are in their rightful place. Harmful spirits cannot invade whole souls, but if there is an imbalance, then their intrusion can lead to illness, or even death. Conversely, the soul of a person, which is often seen to be able to travel independently of a person, especially during dreaming, is subject to fragmentation and what is called *soul loss*, whereby a part goes missing. It is then the healer's job to recover the missing portion and return it to its rightful place inside the person.

In the following section, I provide a number of examples to give a feel for how magical healing is a technique for determining the cause of sickness and affecting a cure. In the process, the ailing person is reintegrated within her community, thereby restoring a harmonious balance of emotional and spiritual equilibrium. To fully understand the importance of a spirit dimension to healing, the anthropologist must get involved with the whole emotional experience, and in the first example, I describe a healing done by a Gypsy shaman to cure my own sickness of spiritual alienation.

## The Spirits of Sickness Know All the Tricks

During the course of an exchange of lengthy letters, I had told a gypsy shaman with whom I was working how I felt cut off from my ancestors; I had forgotten my early connection with my grandfather. It eventually became clear that this was the cause of my sickness: I was spiritually disconnected, and therefore the spirits of sickness could penetrate my body, and he suggested a ritual healing to cure me with the aid of his herbalist assistant.[14]

The three of us sat around a single candle flame, which flickered as we gently rocked in trance to the rhythm of the gypsy's tambourine. A white goose feather and a black crow feather sat on either side of the candle, representing light and dark, and a glass and a bottle of whisky were placed alongside. We had sprinkled salt around and over us as protection against bad spirits. Red wool, also for protection, was tied to our wrists and also hung from the frame of the shaman's tambourine. His herbalist assistant waved a birch wand decorated with a painted green vine interspersed with gold and silver dots, representing the magical otherworld; the small bells tied to the end tinkled to keep away bad spirits.

The shaman, in a controlled spirit possession, was going to channel his spirit ancestor to heal me. Using the rhythm of the tambourine, the shaman allowed his own everyday identity to become malleable—he described it as like dough—thus providing a space for the Ancestor to come through. The shaman rocked backwards and forwards, going deeper and deeper into trance, as the spirit of his ancestor inhabited him. His visage and tone of voice changed, and I sensed a distinct presence in the room. The Ancestor, via the shaman's body, placed his hand on my head and commanded the spirits of sickness to depart—they were told to find their own place and to leave me. All three of us rocked deeper in trance, and the air was thick with emotion. The sound of the jingling wand permeated the atmosphere.

The Ancestor started talking about the spirits of sickness, as he sipped the glass of whisky that had been poured for him:

> The spirits of sickness these days are very comfortable. They know what they can do, they know what they can achieve, and they know all the tricks. So it's a matter of breaking all this down and making them realize that they can't stay here because this life cannot sustain them. They will be far better off going somewhere where they can be as they want to be.

It is the modern attitude that allows the spirits of sickness to invade people; it is this attitude that sees everything as a part of a whole, whereas, by comparison, the old Romani way sees the spirits as separate and external to the self:

> The modern attitude to the spirits of sickness is not a healthy one; sounds quite funny when I say that [laughter]. You need to start to see yourself as being independent from them, so that they can realize they're not a part of you. The spirits of sickness do not realize that they're attacking you; they are such a part of you. They fit quite comfortably; this is their home.
>
> But the old way is not to see it like that. The old way is to see that you and they are very separate. Your modern way has created the condition and so they slot into this quite nicely and feel quite at home.
>
> This is not the way to do it; a change needs to be made and to see them as being very separate spirits . . . Start seeing them as something very separate so that you can start to gradually push them away. It doesn't happen overnight. We ancient ones know this; we know it takes time. Start externalizing these sicknesses that you have and start understanding that they do have their own beings.

The Ancestor told me that I had spent too much time looking at other souls and that this was why the spirits of sickness have found their way into me. I had to believe in myself more, to trust myself and let others find their own way. It was my soul that needed care and attention:

> The way I see your soul, if you'll allow me to say this, [is that] your soul is busy looking into the river but not at its own reflection. Your soul is looking at the reflections of others and seeing their suffering . . . Your own reflection is crying out and is saying 'look at me, look at me'. You need to look into the river and see your own reflection . . . Believe and trust in yourself first and you will find that everything else will slot into place. That is the way of it. That is the way of all souls. That is not simply a Romani way, that is the way of all souls . . . Your soul is what you're looking for . . . You can see to other souls later, and because you are looking at other souls then the spirits of sickness can find their way in because you are not looking or seeing to yourself.

When the Ancestor had had his say, and had drunk his whisky, it was time for him to retreat back into the other world. He said his goodbyes, saying how fond he was of us all. The whole process seemed to be part of an everyday occurrence, as though an elderly and respected relative had just dropped in for a quick drink and a chat. The shaman lay down on the floor while the Ancestor was departing, and after a few minutes, he returned to join in the ordinary conversation that was going on. There was a minimum of fuss as the candle was gently blown out amid laughing and general good humour, as we continued talking into the night.

The ritual was a space where magical consciousness could be focused and deepened and the healing worked on emotional and intuitive levels. The naming of a problem and its personalizing as a spirit of sickness makes an adversarial relationship with it—to name what might be unnameable is empowering. Like divination, it brings unconscious elements of the mind into focus. By focusing on the health of my own soul, by paying it more attention, I could effect my own healing process.

It was after this ritual that everything changed, and I had a spirit communication with my grandfather: he introduced himself as my spirit guide in the realm of the ancestors, and he said that he would look after me. It was then that his storytelling at the magical desk, as I described in Chapter 4, came flooding back in my memory, and I realized his importance to my early life. The effect was profound. I felt a sense of relationship that had previously been missing, and it increased my feeling of connectedness.

## Making the Heart Happy

An important component of magical healing is the process of changing awareness to enter an altered state of consciousness. Such changes in consciousness invite an intimate contact with the spirit world, and this reinforces a shared world view as well as alleviating suffering. In my Romani gypsy ritual, just described, the shaman beat his tambourine, and this sound, plus the tinkling of bells, sent us into a trance; whereas for the Kalahari Kung of southern Africa, the rhythmic clapping of the women leads the men into a healing trance dance.

Four times a month, night signals the start of a community dance, which makes the Kalahari Kung people's 'hearts happy', according to Richard Katz.[15] The women sit around a fire singing and rhythmically clapping, and the men, sometimes joined by the women, dance around the singers. As the dance intensifies, spiritual energy, called *num*, is activated in them, and they begin to experience *kia*, an enhancement of consciousness. All who come are given healing. The healing dances are not separate from the other activities of daily life—dancing, like hunting and gathering, is just another thing that happens—it is, however, a point of marked intensity. The healing dance is open to everyone and to become a healer is to follow a normal pattern of socialization—healing is not the reserve of special persons with extraordinary powers.

Healing may take the form of pulling out a sickness, or of mending the social fabric, as the dance provides for the release of hostility and increases a sense of solidarity, and the dance brings participants into contact with the spirits and gods:

> As midnight approaches with the flickering fire illuminating the singers and
> dancers, a healer or two begins to stagger, then perhaps one falls. They may

shudder or shake violently, their whole body convulsing in apparent pain and anguish. The experience of kia has begun. And then, either on their own or under the guidance of those who are steady, the healers who are in kia go to each person at the dance and begin to heal. They lay their fluttering hands on a person, one hand usually on the chest, the other on the back, pulling out the sickness, while shrieking earth-shattering screams and howls known as *kowhedili*, an expression for the pain and difficulty of this healing work. Then they shake their hands vigorously toward the empty space beyond the dance, casting the sickness they have taken from the person out into the darkness.[16]

Kia comes from the activation of the energy num, which is given by the gods. Activated num is said to boil fiercely within a person, and it is painful and feared. Residing in the pit of the stomach and the base of the spine, the num warms up and becomes a vapour during the dancing; it rises up the spine to the base of the skull and turns into kia, an intense emotional state. Kinachau, an old Kung healer, explains his experience:

> You dance, dance, dance, dance. Then num lifts you up in your belly and lifts you in your back, and you start to shiver. Num makes you tremble; it's hot. Your eyes are open, but you don't look around; you hold your eyes still and look straight ahead. But when you get into kia, you're looking around because you see everything, because you see what's troubling everybody.[17]

Another healer, called 'Kau Dwa', describes the ascent of num: 'in your backbone you feel a pointed something and it works its way up. The base of your spine is tingling, tingling, tingling, tingling. Then num makes your thoughts nothing in your head.'[18] Once heated up, num can both induce kia and combat illness through the pulling out of sickness. According to Kau Dwa, 'when you kia, you see things you must pull out, like the death things that god has put into people. You see people properly, just as they are. Your vision does not whirl.'[19]

During kia, the Kung experience themselves as existing beyond their ordinary level; they can do different things like performing healing, handling and walking on fire and soul travelling to the gods and ancestor spirits. Sickness is seen to be a process whereby the spirits try to take a person to the spirit realm; healing involves a struggle between the spirits of the living and the spirits of the dead. When experiencing kia, they are both beyond themselves and more fully themselves.[20] These rituals have been depicted in rock art, along with other shamanistic activities such as out-of-body travel and transformation into animals, and with drawings of fantastic animals that were killed in the spirit world so that their blood and milk would fall as rain. The sight of the paintings deepened the dancers' trance experiences; power flowed from the images, which were a reservoir of num.[21]

## The Language of the Unconscious

The work of healing with spirits sometimes involves the healer struggling with her own helpful spirits against malevolent ones in the conquest for a person's soul. The manner in which this struggle is experienced is often determined by cultural symbols that organize ways in which the physiological reality of the sickness is perceived and dealt with. The patient may be encouraged to see his illness in terms of a mythic world that is open to sensory, emotional and cognitive manipulation by the healer. The effect of this is to restore a sense of order after the chaos of illness. In his analysis of a Cuna Indian healing song used by a shaman to facilitate a woman's difficult childbirth, anthropologist Claude Lévi-Strauss describes how a shaman battles between helpful and malevolent sprits for the woman's soul. The sick woman believes in the myth, and the society to which she belongs does so, too. The shaman, calling upon myth as a coherent system on which the conception of the universe is founded, will reintegrate the woman into a whole, whereby everything is meaningful, and provide her with a language to express her feelings.[22]

The sick woman has lost one of her souls (*purba*)[23] and therefore her vital strength (*niga*).[24] The shaman, assisted by his spirit helpers, undertakes a journey to the spirit world to snatch the soul from the malevolent spirit that has captured it. When he restores it to the woman, she is cured. The *abode of Muu* represents the vagina and uterus of the pregnant woman, and it is within the vagina and the uterus that the spirit combat is conducted. Muu is an instigator of disorder—a special soul that has captured and paralyzed the other special souls, thus destroying the cooperation of the integrity of the body and its vital strength. Muu is not an evil force, but rather, a force gone awry.

The shaman retrieves the soul of the heart, bones, teeth, hair, nails and feet, but not the soul of the uterus or the vagina, because Muu, the soul of these organs, is not a victim, but rather, is responsible for the pathological disorder. In this difficult delivery, the soul of the uterus has led other souls astray. Mobilizing the lords of the wild animals to guard the way so that Muu cannot escape, the shaman must follow 'Muu's way'—the vagina of the sick woman. The shaman sings the following song (in English translation):

> The (sick) woman lies in the hammock in front of you.
> Her white tissue lies in her lap, her white tissues move softly.
> The (sick) woman's body lies weak.
> When they light up (along) Muu's way, it runs
> over with exudations and like blood.
> Her exudations drip down below the hammock
> All like blood, all red.

The inner white tissue extends to the bosom of the earth.

Into the middle of the woman's white tissue a human being descends.[25]

The 'white inner tissue' refers to the woman's vulva, and 'Muu's way' is darkened and completely covered in blood due to the difficult labour.

The song populates the uterine world full of fantastic monsters and dangerous animals, and these personify the pain, presenting to the woman a form accessible to conscious or unconscious thought: 'Uncle Alligator, who moves about with his bulging eyes, his striped and variegated body, crouching and wriggling his tail', and 'he-who-has-a-hat-that-is-soft' and the guardian animals black tiger, the red animal and so on. The shaman has to overcome these obstacles as well as fibres, loose threads, fastened threads and successive curtains that are rainbow coloured, golden, silvery, white and wormlike. After the souls are liberated, the shaman must descend. For the descent, which is just as dangerous as the ascent, the shaman summons reinforcements of the 'clearers of the way' and animals such as armadillo.

Then the shaman leaves for the mountains with people of the village to gather medicinal plants. When he returns, he imitates a penis and penetrates the 'opening of Muu' and calls for the help of a people of Bowmen, who raise a cloud of dust to 'obscure . . . Muu's way' and defend all of Muu's crossroads and byroads. The cure lies in making explicit a situation originally existing on an emotional level and 'rendering acceptable to the mind pains which the body refuses to tolerate'.[26]

This language is, for Lévi-Strauss, the language of the unconscious, and in this view, he shows the influence of psychologist Sigmund Freud, as we saw in Chapter 5. Freud founded psychoanalysis as a therapeutic technique for understanding unconscious repressions and bringing them to consciousness, and it was Freud's way of reaching aspects of mind ignored by the biomedical model. Psychoanalysis developed from Freud's study of altered states of consciousness. Freud initially used seances and hypnotic trance as a means of curing psychosomatic illness. He used techniques of suggestion when people were in trance; this bypassed the so-called gating mechanism within the brain that controls the input. It was thought that images from the unconscious only emerged within a jumbled form, as in dreams, because they would be too distressing if not filtered by the gating mechanism. Freud eventually turned to dream interpretation as another means of penetrating the hidden areas of the unconscious.

Lévi-Strauss explored Freud's approach, and he makes a parallel between shamanistic and psychoanalytic healing. Both are means to express the inexpressible, and both induce an experience by re-creating a myth that, according to Lévi-Strauss, reaches a universal unconscious mind. The difference is that the shamanistic healing uses a collective myth, whereas psychoanalysis is personal to the individual:

| Shamanistic Healing | Psychoanalysis |
|---|---|
| Mythic language (collective) | Mythic language (personal) |
| Action through spirits | Access to the unconscious |

Lévi-Strauss's view is to see the collective mythic language of shamanism as accessing the unconscious mind, but once more, as in his logical interpretation of myth in Chapter 5, there is no room for a spirit component.

## Seeing the Spirit

Unlike Lévi-Strauss, anthropologist Edith Turner acknowledges the importance of a spirit dimension in healing by immersing herself in the experience of a curative ritual. The profound impact of the experience led Turner to realize that it demanded a reorganization of the way she did anthropology. The role of the anthropologist was to 'tell the story', as she was part of the process. Healing involved the bringing together of varying meaningful aspects of life for all of the participants. The magical experience demands that the anthropologist get more involved in her own emotional experience: to shift awareness from analytical thinking to a more magical mode of mind.

Turner had returned to Zambia to do more fieldwork among the Ndembu, a matrilineal people living in what was once high savannah forest. First visiting the area with husband and anthropologist Victor Turner thirty-one years earlier,[27] she noted that curative rituals were now on the upgrade and that almost at once, opportunities for participation came her way. Perceiving that African curing had been passing through an exploratory experimental stage, where it was impossible for the official medical authorities to hamper it, she made the acquaintance of a couple of *ihamba* spirit doctors, and she, and her assistant, were invited to a curing ritual, with Turner being appointed as one of the doctors due to her previous experience. Turner's account of the removal of a bad spirit in the form of *ihamba*, a dead hunter's tooth, which wandered around a sick woman's body, causing pain, involved searching for medicinal plants, a spirit communication with ancestors, the preparation of medicines, a bringing together of the social group with the release of emotions and grudges and the drawing out of a harmful spirit in the patient.

Helping to search for medicines that come from special trees and plants that have power, Turner describes how the doctors came to an African oak whose name means 'the gathering together of a herd of animals'. She described how Singleton, one of the doctors, approached the tree:

> Singleton hunkered down before the base of the tree and took his mongoose skin bag from which he drew a lump of red clay which he rubbed in a broad line down the west side of the trunk, then in a line from the foot of the tree to himself, and finally down the east side of the tree. He drew the lines to call ihamba (the tooth spirit) to come soon—to direct ihamba along the lines. Singleton told us, 'Ihamba knows "I am soon going to be out of the patient"?'. (Singleton saw the tooth-spirit as a conscious being.) Then Singleton took a cup of beer and poured it out at the foot of the tree, on both sides, saying loudly and abruptly, 'Maheza!'
> 'Maheza!' we shouted back.
> 'Ngambu!'
> 'Yafwa!' we returned.[28]

Singleton recited the names of his healer ancestors who have handed down the ritual and then was told what to do by the spirit of his father and the others. The healing party went on to gather other medicines from other plants for the ritual.

The medicines were prepared by pounding the leaves and mixing them with water, while people gathered for the ritual. One portion was left to make a cold tea, and another was heated on a fire. The healers drank the tea. Tasting it, Turner commented, 'For a moment it made my head swim, but soon my senses cleared.' Meru, the sick woman, was washed with the medicines; the pounded leaves were squeezed onto her body until she was entirely drenched with them, to 'open her from the outside'. The doctors used red clay to draw a line down her brow and nose, temples and cheekbones to protect her head. Then they gave her medicines to drink to 'open her from the inside'.[29]

Amid drumming and the shouting of 'Come out!' to the spirit inside Meru's body, the doctors made tiny slits in her back, sucking on cupping horns and shouting to the spirit to come out. Meru said that she wanted to die because there was no one to look after her—all her children had died. Words were spoken in a high, oratorical tone that reiterated all her complaints; all resentments and bitterness were aired. Grudges were brought out: a sister did not give her the full price for some beer that she had brewed. Meru fell shaking in the midst of the singing. The doctor tried to draw out the spirit tooth.

Turner reported that she, as anthropologist, was overcome with emotion when someone accused her of not visiting when she said she would. She was expected to say 'words', and she wanted to participate, but she could not, and she cried, and through her tears she could see Meru swaying; the barriers were breaking, and she felt the spiritual motion: 'it was a tangible feeling of breakthrough encompassing the entire group.'[30] The spirit tooth was drawn out of Meru's body, and Turner recorded it thus:

Amid the bellow of the drums, Singleton swooped rhythmically with his finger horn and skin bag, ready to catch the tooth. Bill [Turner's assistant] beat the side of the drum in time to the rhythm, and as for me, I had just found out how to clap. You simply clap with the drums, and clap *hard*. All the rest falls into place. Your whole body becomes deeply involved in the rhythm, and all reaches a unity. Singleton was at Meru's side and the crowd was on its feet clapping. Singleton pressed Meru's back, guiding and leading out the tooth— Meru's face in a grin of tranced passion, her back quivering rapidly.

Suddenly Meru raised her arm, stretched it in liberation, and I saw with my own eyes a giant thing emerging out of the flesh of her back. It was a large gray blob about six inches across, opaque and something between solid and smoke.[31]

Although she did not come out with any 'words' like the rest of the group, Turner said that her tears were obvious, and that they were a 'kind of language'; she was part of the release that came from what was happening to everyone together. The emotional release united all in a feeling of cconnectedness, between individuals, ancestors and the social community.

Turner was amazed and delighted to have seen ihamba, and she recounts that she still laughs with glee at the realization of having seen it: 'the gray thing was actually out there, visible, and you could see Singleton's hands working and scrabbling on the back. And then it was there no more. Singleton had whatever it was in his pouch, pressing it in with his other hand. The receiving can was ready; he transferred whatever it was into it and capped the castor oil leaf and bark lid over. It was done.'[32] The spirit was seen as a conscious being that was being drawn out of the sick patient; this is incomprehensible to materialists (those who do not recognize the substantive reality of the spiritual dimension).

Magical healing cannot be fully understood from a materialist perspective; with ordinary, everyday vision, the spirit of sickness could not be seen. However, in a state of heightened emotion, consciousness changes, and many people, like Turner, can see psychic emanations. Others may have other intense sensory awareness—of hearing, smell or taste. Some shamans use such a strongly developed sense for curing. One example of this is Essie Parrish, a Native American shamanic healer from the Pomo tribe of northern California, who explained to anthropologist Barbara Tedlock how she could hear the sound of illness like insects, as recounted from a dream:

In her dream she sang the song as she walked in sunlit hills and valleys that were not of this world. She came to a crossroads and turned east along a narrow path between sparkling multi-colored flowers covered with monarch butterflies. When she reached the end, she saw silken strands woven into a web filled with tiny gemstones. As she looked closer she saw bits of turquoise, abalone, and jet swirling around a central white light. Then she heard a raspy noise, something like a cricket, and realized it was the sound of illness.

'Dangerous beings we call "in-dwellers" are living inside our bodies like insects, like ants,' she whispered. 'When I sing I can see where they're hiding in their nests. I massage that area and scatter them in all directions.'[33]

The disease pulls her hands like magnets, and she sucks it out, as Essie explains:

My middle finger is the one with the power. When I work with my hands it's just like when you cast for fish and they tug on your bait. The pain sitting somewhere inside feels like it's pulling your hand toward itself—you can't miss it. No way. It even lets you touch it!

I don't place my hands myself. It feels like someone, the disease perhaps, is pulling me. It's something like a magnet.

When power touches the pain you gasp. Your throat closes you simply can't breathe when your breath is shut off like that it feels as if your chest were paralyzed. If you should breathe while holding that pain, the disease could hide itself.

As you quiet your breathing you can feel the pain and your hand can take it out. But if you are afraid and your breathing is not shut off, you can't lift out the pain.

When I take it out you can't see it with your bare eyes. But I can see it . . .

The palm of my hand also heals. But it doesn't work just anytime: only when I summon power. If there are people who are sick somewhere, my hands find them. Whenever someone thinks toward me, there on the tip of my middle finger it acts as if shot. If you touch electricity, you'll know what it's like. . .

I found the pain with my hand and sucked it out. Something like a bubble came up out of my throat. Just as it would if you blew up a big balloon, that's how it came from my mouth. Everyone there saw it. It had become inflated quite a lot when it floated from my mouth, like foaming bubbles.

Ever since then I've been sucking out illness. This place right here [pointing to the midpoint of her neck] is where the power enters my throat. The disease acts as fast as a lightening bolt striking a tree. It acts in a flash, shutting off the breath. One doesn't notice how long one holds one's breath. It's like being in what white people call a trance.

While the disease is coming to me, I'm in a trance. It speaks to me firmly saying, 'This is the way it is. It is such and such a kind of disease. This is why that person is sick.' But when I come out of the trance I no longer remember what the disease told me.[34]

Both divination and magical healing involve techniques of changing consciousness to enable participants to experience an expanded state of mind, and it is within this experience that a restructuring of lived reality can take place. In the case of divination, answers to problems or questions may become evident; whereas in healing, there is a change in relationship between the sick person and her disease as well as between the sick person and her community. The spirit dimension of everyday life is obviously a powerful one. It is a difficult one for anthropology because it threatens to undermine the discipline's scientific foundations. In the next chapter, we turn to an examination of the very issue of the reality of spirits.

## NOTES

1. Tanya Luhrmann, *Persuasions of the Witch's Craft: Ritual Magic and Witchcraft in Present-Day England* (Cambridge: Basil Blackwell, 1989), p. 151.
2. Barbara Tedlock, 'Divination as a Way of Knowing: Embodiment, Visualisation, Narrative and Interpretation', *Folklore* (Oct. 2001), http://findarticles.com/p/articles/mi_m2386/is_2_112/ai_79548472/, accessed 26 March 2009.
3. Barbara Tedlock, 'Toward a Divinatory Practice', *Anthropology of Consciousness*, 17 (2006), pp. 62–77.
4. Frank Speck, *Naskapi* (Norman: University of Oklahoma Press, 1935), p. 150; cited in Omar Khayyam Moore, 'Divination—a New Perspective', in William A. Lessa and Evon Z. Vogt, eds, *Reader in Comparative Religion: An Anthropological Approach*, 4th ed. (New York: Harper and Row, 1979), p. 377.
5. Tedlock, 'Divination as a Way of Knowing'.
6. Valerie I. J. Flint, *The Rise of Magic in Early Medieval Europe* (Oxford: Clarendon Press, 1991), p. 103.
7. Flint, *Rise of Magic*, pp. 160–1.
8. Flint, *Rise of Magic*, p. 88.
9. Owen Davies, *Witchcraft, Magic and Culture 1736–1951* (Manchester: Manchester University Press, 1999), p. 214.
10. 'Astrology in the White House', *Time* (16 May 1988).
11. Richard Katz, *Boiling Energy: Community Healing among the Kalahari Kung* (Cambridge, MA: Harvard University Press, 1982), p. 33.
12. Barbara Tedlock, *The Woman in the Shaman's Body: Reclaiming the Feminine in Religion and Medicine* (New York: Bantam, 2005), pp. 15–16.
13. Elliott Dacher, 'The Whole Healing System', http://www.healthy.net/scr/Article.asp?Id=2142, accessed 26 March 2009.
14. See Susan Greenwood, *The Nature of Magic* (Oxford: Berg, 2005), pp. 111–17, for a fuller account.
15. Richard Katz, *Boiling Energy*, p. 34.
16. Richard Katz, *Boiling Energy*, pp. 35–6, 40.
17. Richard Katz, *Boiling Energy*.
18. Richard Katz, *Boiling Energy*.
19. Richard Katz, *Boiling Energy*.
20. Richard Katz, *Boiling Energy*, p. 43.
21. J. D. Lewis-Williams, 'Southern African Shamanistic Rock Art in Its Social and Cognitive Contexts', in Neil Price, ed., *The Archaeology of Shamanism* (London: Routledge, 2001), pp. 22, 34.

22. Claude Lévi-Strauss, 'The Effectiveness of Symbols', in Lessa and Vogt, *Reader in Comparative Religion*, pp. 323–4; reprinted from Claude Lévi-Strauss, *Structural Anthropology* (New York: Basic Books, 1963).

23. *Purba* is 'double' or 'soul'—plants and stones have a *purba*, but not a *niga*; each part of the body has its own *purba*, which governs its functions.

24. *Niga* is the vitality of the whole organism that develops with age.

25. Lévi-Strauss, 'The Effectiveness of Symbols', p. 319.

26. Lévi-Strauss, 'The Effectiveness of Symbols', p. 323.

27. See Victor Turner, *Schism and Continuity in an African Society: A Study of Ndembu Village Life* (Manchester: Manchester University Press, 1957); *The Forest of Symbols: Aspects of Ndembu Ritual* (Ithaca: Cornell University Press, 1967); *The Drums of Affliction: A Study of Religious Processes among the Ndembu of Zambia* (Oxford: Clarendon Press, 1968); *Revelation and Divination in Ndembu Ritual* (Ithaca: Cornell University Press, 1975).

28. Edith Turner, 'A Visible Spirit Form in Zambia', in David E. Young and Jean-Guy Goulet, eds, *Being Changed by Cross-Cultural Encounters: The Anthropology of Extraordinary Experience* (Toronto: Broadview Press, 1994), pp. 75–6.

29. Turner, 'A Visible Spirit Form', p. 80.

30. Turner, 'A Visible Spirit Form', p. 83.

31. Turner, 'A Visible Spirit Form', p. 83.

32. Turner, 'A Visible Spirit Form', pp. 83–5.

33. Tedlock, *Woman in the Shaman's Body*, pp. 17–18.

34. Tedlock, *Woman in the Shaman's Body*, pp. 17–19.

## FURTHER READING

Greenwood, Susan, 'Magical Identity: Healing and Powers, Chapter 5, in *Magic, Witchcraft and the Otherworld*, Oxford: Berg 2000, pp. 117–149.

Katz, Richard, *Boiling Energy: Community Healing among the Kalahari Kung*, Cambridge, MA: Harvard University Press, 1982.

Kottler, Jeffrey A., and Jon Carlson (with Bradford Keeney), *American Shaman: An Odyssey of Global Healing Traditions*. New York: Brunner-Routledge, 2004.

Tedlock, Barbara, 'Divination as a Way of Knowing: Embodiment, Visualisation, Narrative, and Interpretation', *Folklore* (Oct. 2001), http://findarticles.com/p/articles/mi_m2386/is_2_112/ai_79548472/, accessed 26 March 2009.

Tedlock, Barbara, *The Woman in the Shaman's Body: Reclaiming the Feminine in Religion and Medicine*. New York: Bantam Books, 2006.

Turner, Edith, 'A Visible Spirit Form in Zambia', in David E. Young and Jean-Guy Goulet, eds, *Being Changed by Cross-Cultural Encounters: The Anthropology of Extraordinary Experience*, Toronto: Broadview Press, 1994, pp. 72–6.

# SECTION FOUR
# WORKING WITH MAGIC

To reach a peak experience in a ritual, it really is necessary to sink oneself fully in it. Thus for me, 'going native' achieved a breakthrough to an altogether different worldview, foreign to academia, by means of which certain material was chronicled that could have been gathered in no other way.[1]

—Edith Turner

Our mind experiences discomfort, confusion and perplexity: what is a world which is not rational and intelligible? And it gets out of it by saying: it is a world which is not real (imaginary, arbitrary, fabulous, like fairy stories).[2]

—Lucien Lévy-Bruhl

The mind contains no things, no pigs, no people, no midwife toad, or what have you, only ideas (i.e., news of difference), information about 'things' in quotes, always in quotes. Similarly, the mind contains no time and no space, only ideas of 'time' and 'space.'[3]

—Gregory Bateson

Anthropologists working in the field encounter specific challenges when confronted with the gap between informants' accounts of spirit beings and their own position as researchers within the essentially rationalistic academic anthropological discipline. Magic poses problems for many anthropologists; this is due to the fact that its spiritual nature conflicts with Western notions of rationality, as we will see in Chapter 8. A more inclusive scientific framework is needed that overcomes the theoretical tendency to devalue magical experience and to recognize magical knowledge as a valuable aspect of human consciousness. Chapter 9 builds on ideas developed by Gregory Bateson and Geoffrey Samuel to just this end.

# 8   THE NATURE OF REALITY

Vincent Crapanzano tells of a Moroccan tile maker, Tuhami, who was married to 'A'isha Qandisha, a *jinniyya*, a camel-footed she-demon with a hag and a seductive beauty aspect. Tuhami's marriage to the jinniyya represented for Crapanzano the confrontation with the exotic, the bizarre and the mad. Was she the product of Tuhami's imagination, a projection or a collective representation? Was she not quite real? He asks whether we look to 'reality' to understand, without questioning the status of that reality.[4] Tuhami's marriage to a spirit is a problem for science. Anthropology as a social science has been subject to the constraints of the natural sciences, in theory, if not always in practice. The history of the development of science has shown a sustained emphasis on reason, rationality and the separation of the thinking mind from a lifeless matter. In these respects, anthropology has tried to be more so-called scientific than some of the natural sciences. A recognition of difference is threatening; it may produce what Crapanzano calls *epistemological vertigo*,[5] and the difference may make us feel dizzy.[6] However, wittingly or unwittingly, says Crapanzano, the anthropologist (or her reader) often causes difference to disappear in the process of translation, or alternatively, such translation may render bizarre, exotic or downright irrational what would have been ordinary in its own context. The ethnography for Westerners versed in scientific materialism may come to represent what Crapanzano describes as 'a sort of allegorical anti-world, similar to the anti-worlds of the insane and the child'.[7]

Writing about spirits makes Crapanzano feel uncomfortable. Describing the ethnographic engagement as a 'complex negotiation in which the parties to the encounter acquiesce to a certain reality', Crapanzano describes the spirit marriage with 'uneasiness and a certain regret' because Tuhami becomes a figure within an imposed allegory that bypasses him—the presence of the ethnographer allows Tuhami to tell his story to a rationalizing science.[8] Such a science tends to ignore the experience, the personal and what it calls 'the irrational', and it is this that makes Crapanzano point out that Westerners should question their fundamental assumptions about the nature of reality.

This is exactly what Edith Turner has done in her advocacy of a more open approach to experiencing and understanding spirits, as demonstrated in the last chapter, when she wrote about her whole body becoming so deeply emotionally involved that she could see the ihamba spirit tooth. This made Turner rethink her role as anthropologist. She describes how anthropologists used to view such participation in the middle of the twentieth century:

> In the past in anthropology, if a researcher 'went native', it doomed him academically. My husband, Victor Turner, and I had this dictum at the back of our minds when we spent two and a half years among the Ndembu of Zambia in the fifties. All right, 'our' people believed in spirits, but that was a matter of their different world, not ours. Their ideas were strange and a little disturbing, but somehow we were on the safe side of the white divide and were free merely to study the beliefs. This is how we thought. Little knowing it, we denied the people's equality with ours, their 'coevalness', their common humanity as that humanity extended itself into the spirit world. Try out that spirit world ourselves? No way.[9]

Fortunately, academic opinion has moved on since then, and anthropologists, such as Victor and Edith Turner, have examined the anthropology of experience.[10] Victor Turner, influenced by German philosopher Wilhem Dilthey (1833–1911) and American philosopher and psychologist John Dewey (1859–1952), wrote that of all the human sciences and studies, anthropology was the 'most deeply rooted in social and subjective experience of the inquirer'. He further went on to say that 'all human act is impregnated with meaning and meaning is hard to measure, though it can often be grasped, even if only fleetingly and ambiguously'.[11]

After the death of her husband, Edith Turner started to develop the experiential aspects of anthropological experience using altered states of consciousness, following the lead given by anthropologist Michael Harner. Initially conducting fieldwork among the Jívaro and Conibo Indians between 1956 and 1961, Harner then went on to develop a system of techniques, mainly based on rhythmic drumming, that introduced shamanism to Westerners without the use of the psychotropic substances that he had encountered whilst in the field.[12] Edith Turner attended one of Harner's workshops and learnt how to visualise during a journey in 1987, and this gave her the skills to start exploring her own consciousness.[13]

It was Harner's technique of journeying as a form of active meditation to the beat of a drum that enabled me also to explore magical consciousness through my own experiences such as the communication with a spirit owl described in the introduction to this book. Harner describes the type of experience that can be gained from such journeys as an ancient human legacy, one that Westerners have been cut off from for centuries.[14] Such experiences are a feature of the human condition and typically immerse the participant in a world alive with spirits.

*Spirit* is a term with diverse meanings—it can refer to the inward, nonmaterial part of a person or 'soul'; a being not connected with a material body, a disembodied soul or incorporeal beings such as a jinniyya, an elf or a fairy; or it can refer to the innate quality or essence of a person, for example we say that a person has courage, vivacity or indeed 'spirituality', or he may lack vigour and be called 'despirited' or spiritless. Spirits are minimal creatures, shadows, the unfocussed—things that are hard to grasp by analytic reason.[15] In most cultures, various categories of phenomena are distinguished from common sense reality. These categories are associated with a realm of uncanny mind-bearing beings, whose power, logical status and relationships to space and time are different from those of humans in the ordinary social world.[16] *Spiritual* implies nonmateriality, as in the Cartesian division between mind (spirit) and body (matter), as we will see later in this chapter. Spiritual represents the opposite of material existence; a more subtle mode of corporeal existence[17] that cannot usually be seen, except under certain conditions and in trance, as we saw in the last chapter. Seeing spirits as real can be disorientating for Westerners versed in scientific rationalism, and the experience is often denied, as Lévy-Bruhl has pointed out: 'our mind experiences discomfort, confusion and perplexity: what is a world which is not rational and intelligible? And it gets out of it by saying: it is a world which is not real (imaginary, arbitrary, fabulous, like fairy stories).'[18] Although perhaps for the general population, a spiritual world is never very far away—for example in newspaper astrological predictions or stars and a whole range of alternative therapies such as spirit healing and homeopathy—but for social scientists versed in rationalistic discourses and theories, such a world is remote, if not nonexistent.

## QUESTIONING WESTERN ASSUMPTIONS ABOUT SPIRITS

How can we begin to examine an inspirited reality? We need to question, as Crapanzano has suggested, our unexamined assumptions about the nature of reality. In Western cultures, the analytical mode of consciousness asks questions about whether spirits are real, and this is interesting in itself in relation to their social and psychological effects, but it does not help us understand the nature of reality and how our conception of spirits might fit into that.

An early definition of religion posed by Edward Tylor focused on religion being a belief in spirit beings. Edward Tylor coined the term *animism* to describe an inspirited world by putting an emphasis on the soul, as the spiritual aspect of a person, in early anthropological discussions on the origins of religious beliefs. He thought that primitive reflection on death, disease, trances, visions and dreams was accounted for by the presence or absence of a soul (spirit). Eventually, he thought, this view became transferred onto other creatures and inanimate objects, too. The soul was independent of its material home, and the idea about spiritual beings arose and eventually developed into notions of gods.[19] Tylor also thought that beliefs about spirits would gradually be replaced by science in the evolution of human thought, thus rendering such notions obsolete. This evolutionary view is now outmoded; however, its legacy lingers on in anthropological understandings of spirit. So how can we develop our understanding of spirit without losing our scientific objectivity?

A key to answering that question, and other questions posed here of whether the spirit was the product of Tuhami's imagination, or a projection, or a collective representation, or whether she was real, lies in understanding magic as a mode of consciousness. To do this, we have to step outside of the Western view of reality that dismisses the idea that spirits are real. Before we can do that, however, we need to understand two key underlying factors that shape Western assumptions about the nature of reality. The first shows how the historical development of science in the seventeenth century came to exclude a spirit world by co-opting the practical and experimental aspects of magic and rejecting its spiritual dimension; and the second outlines the Cartesian philosophy of the separation of spirit matter, whereby the living world came to be seen in mechanistic terms.

### The Irrationality of Magic

In the seventeenth century, during what has come to be termed the *scientific revolution*, the practical experimental aspects of magic were absorbed into science, leaving other spiritual features of magic to be denounced as irrational. The shift from a magical view, in which there was no division between spirit and matter, to a rational pursuit of science involved the material and immaterial aspects of natural philosophy becoming separated. Natural philosophy was a complete system that incorporated spirit and matter—with disciplinary traditions ranging from astronomy, mechanics, anatomy, medicine, metaphysics, pharmacology, cartography, mining and metallurgy to optics, music and physiology, amongst others—and that aimed to describe the entire system of the world. At the time of the scientific revolution, there was no concept of science, the present use of the word being first coined in the nineteenth century.[20]

The scientific world view developed partly out of a marriage of natural philosophy and the pragmatic and empirical tradition of sympathetic magic. Natural philosophy, as defined by Galilei Galileo (1564–1642), an Italian physicist, astronomer and philosopher; Auguste Comte (1798–1857), a French philosopher; and the English naturalist Charles Darwin (1809–1882), concerned a pursuit of objective knowledge of phenomena.[21] As we saw in Chapter 3, magic was chiefly concerned with exploiting the sympathies and antipathies between corresponding things. Based on an assumption that certain things had hidden or occult powers to affect other things, natural magic was dependent on a profound knowledge of how to use these powers to achieve a desired outcome. A reforming natural philosophy denounced magic and, at the same time, took what was useful.[22]

Francis Bacon was one of the first natural philosophers to advocate the experimental method as the most reliable way of acquiring knowledge of the natural world. Rationalist and speculative natural philosophy and experimental natural magic had once been completely separate traditions, but Bacon advocated the use of the experimental method of the magician in a reformed natural philosophy. The good ideas in magic were silently incorporated into reformed natural knowledge, while the bad ideas were used to denounce magic as a sink of false and ludicrous beliefs.[23]

Magical traditions played an important part in the major shift from scholastic natural philosophy to the new, more practically useful empirical natural philosophy of the scientific revolution. As historian John Henry notes, 'the history of magic since the eighteenth century has been the history of what was left of that tradition *after* major elements of natural magic had been absorbed into natural philosophy.'[24] Natural magic disappeared from the Western conception of magic due to its most fundamental aspects being co-opted. This had a major impact on how magic is viewed in academia, even amongst historians of science, a number of which have, dismissed what they see as the irrational. This view tends to ignore the depth and complexity of the magical tradition and further supports a division between magic and science.[25]

During this period, the course was set for the advancement of causal logic over magical thinking, and these ideas reached their full expression during the eighteenth-century Enlightenment, a time when occult phenomena were no longer significant as a form of explanation and were deemed mere superstition, a relic of a dark and primitive past.

As the term suggests, the period saw greater light shed on the conduct of human affairs: the dark mysteries of traditional attitudes in religion and political life were pushed back, and in their place a new outlook grew up, informed by reason and the power of scientific research and discovery.[26] God had created the world as a perfect, rational machine. Humans could become part of this rationality through the knowledge of the self-perfection of God's design; if God's laws of nature were rational, then it was through reason that people could discover them. The global effort of the Enlightenment was to explain other religions as false, and the beliefs of other societies were seen as primitive, backward and unenlightened.[27]

## Separating Spirit from Matter

Much of this view of science derives from the work of seventeenth-century philosopher René Descartes (1596–1650), who had an ecstatic visionary experience, during which the nature of the universe was revealed to him. Rather ironically, Descartes became convinced that his mission in life was to seek truth by reason. Putting an emphasis on reason as the basis of analytic knowledge, he argued that truth was derived from rational reflection, rather than from experience and observation of the senses. A mathematician at the outset of his career, working on music, optics and mechanics,[28] Descartes is famous for his cogito 'I think, therefore I am'. Descartes thought that ideas came from thinking itself: the mind produced ideas out of its own processes of rational reflection on the world. Ideas such as this often have an unconscious impact, and this cogito shapes an attitude of mind over matter, meaning that it is important to rise above the experience. If you know this maxim, then you know Descartes's main idea. He separated the thinking mind, which had a soul, from mechanistic, soulless matter. The mind, for Descartes, was a thinking substance with an immaterial soul capable of self-consciousness. By contrast, the body was material and part of the mechanistic universe; it had no soul and no consciousness, and it was under the control of its emotions and external stimuli. A soul without a body would have consciousness, but only of innate ideas, lacking sensory impressions of the world[29]:

| Thinking Mind | Mechanistic Matter |
|---|---|
| Spirit (soul) | Material |
| Consciousness | No consciousness |

Unifying maths and physics, Descartes sought to show how the new philosophy could explain the forms, functions and vital processes of living creatures through mechanistic accounts. His starting point was to draw on William Harvey's work on the heart and blood and excise it of its vitalistic elements.[30] Descartes's mechanical philosophy was highly influential, and it was forged out of his attempts to understand the world upon certainties of geometrical reasoning. Descartes's work contributed to the mathematization of the world picture, and his mechanical philosophy marked a definite break with the past and set the seal upon how science would come to be seen.[31]

Descartes's legacy was the separation of spirit (mind) from matter, and this notion has had an abiding influence on Western culture—it is thought, rather than experience of the senses, that is valued. However, Descartes was not the first thinker in this rationalist tradition. We have already seen how, for Plato, the senses were untrustworthy (Chapter 2). The valuing of reason over experience has not been helpful for understanding magic, and the Cartesian legacy shaped Western notions of science, its rationalism still evident in anthropological thinking today. Magic is now contrasted with the Western style of thought, which firmly locates knowledge of the world in science. A division has occurred between a rational science identified with the material world, on one hand, and magic, looming large as an irrational belief in spirits, on the other. Magic is misunderstood and trivialized by the belief that only the naive take it seriously, or that it is only the practice of charlatans or evil-doers.

These views fail to give the full picture of the role of magic in culture or history.[32] Magic has become a collect-all term for all that is unorthodox, irrational or just inexplicable. The separation of spirit from matter left a world that was despirited, and this corresponded with the development of science as a rationalistic pursuit.

### Outlandish, Apparently Irrational Beliefs

One such example of a perspective that equates knowledge of the world with reason and rationality is a study of contemporary Western magic undertaken by Tanya Luhrmann during the 1980s. Unfortunately, even though she looked at psychological aspects of magical belief, Luhrmann rendered the dynamics of magic invisible. Luhrmann asked how modern Westerners, with a knowledge of science, could believe in magic. Like Frazer, Luhrmann is ultimately dismissive of magic as a source of knowledge because it does not conform to her positivistic notions of scientific truth. Positivism is a philosophical outlook that exalts the sciences as providing the only valid tools for acquiring knowledge of the world; in this view, magic is irrational. The sciences are based on the process of induction from occurrences in the visible, tangible world, and ideas about unobservable entities, often associated with explanations of why things happen, are not essential to the process of scientific investigation.[33]

Luhrmann described what she calls a *multifarious occult*, a mixture of many different activities and ideas such as paganism, astrology, mysticism, a range of alternative therapies and Kabbalism (Jewish mysticism), and her focus was on how these people accepted 'outlandish, apparently irrational beliefs',[34] and how they came to make certain assertions and to act as if they were true. Her broad question was on the nature of rationality and irrationality and the basic form of human cognition. She wanted to explore the ways in which people systematically departed from some clean-shaven, rational ideal. The purpose of her research was to examine how apparently rational people came to engage with irrational beliefs, and to identify the elements that seemed important to an explanation of how they came to hold these views.[35]

Luhrmann's goal was to describe the process by which the business of engaging in magic became reasonable to its practitioners.[36] To do this, she employed what she termed *interpretive drift* to describe the 'slow, often unacknowledged shift in someone's manner of interpreting events' as he became more involved with his experiences of magical practice.[37] Interpretive drift involved the bringing together of interpretation, experience and rationalization to create a shift in a magician's basic perception and analysis of events; the process brought experiential changes in psychological, emotional and physiological areas of life and also induced a person to rationalize the disjunction between magic and a scientific way of understanding.[38] Newcomers become progressively more skilled at seeing patterns in events, seeing certain sorts of events as significant and paying attention to new patterns[39] using magical correspondences, planets, colours, gods and goddesses, incense, days of the week and archangels.

These magicians used astrology and tarot for divination, and this formed part of what Luhrmann called their common knowledge, the tools for insight consisting of organized sets of symbols and myths that changed the magicians' ways of seeing patterns and connections between events. Common knowledge was not a body of precise facts, but rather, something Luhrmann saw as 'fuzzier' and ambiguous.[40] Magicians developed a 'feel' for what each card meant by grasping the 'sense'—a fuzzy, often unverbalized awareness—of the card and interpreting the pattern that they saw in a spread of cards that retained the sense.[41] The 'fuzzy' sense and the pattern that she was talking about is the expanded awareness of magical consciousness. Luhrmann did not consider that the 'fuzzy' sense that she described had any real value in itself; it was just part of a process of rationalization of interpretative drift—making the irrational practice of magic acceptable in a departure from reason. At this point, it is worth comparing my approach to tarot and divination in Chapter 7. Luhrmann's work does not get us far in an understanding of the process of mind that experiences spirits as real, and we will now turn to alternative explanations that do not reduce magical experience to the method of a rationalized science.

## A STREAM OF CONSCIOUSNESS

Causality and participation, as two coexisting orientations to the world (see Chapter 2), can potentially both be experienced within any individual and examined as aspects, or modes, of human consciousness. In his book *Principles of Psychology* (first published in 1890), American psychologist and philosopher William James (1842–1910) describes consciousness as being like a stream or river; it is a continuous and always changing process, whereby some parts are in focus, while others are excluded. James sees the mind as a 'theatre of simultaneous possibilities', in which consciousness is a process that compares, selects and suppresses data, much as a sculptor works on a block of stone, extricating one interpretation from the rest. He writes that 'my world is but one in a million alike embedded, alike real to those who may abstract them'.[42] The picture that emerges from James's view is that there is a multiplicity of aspects of consciousness, rather than a single state. We each have our own *experience* of consciousness: our perceptions of the world, thoughts, ideas, beliefs, values, feelings, emotions, fears and dreams.

William James's ideas had a great influence on anthropologists, for example Malinowski's theory of magic, which identified the universal magical use of language, was inspired by James,[43] and Evans-Pritchard, drawing on the work of James, observes that we are aware of only a small part of all the stream of sensory information that connects with our senses. Some aspects of this stream we are conscious of, and though some aspects may not be conscious, they have been 'noticed' by our senses. Any sound or sight may reach the brain of a person without entering into consciousness—a person may 'hear' or 'see' something but not notice it.[44] In a stream of sense impressions, it is not surprising, then, that only a few become conscious emotional impressions, and society directs the individual's attention to them by collectively deciding and training us, as we grow up and become enculturated, that some are more important than others. Hence, in a science-based society, the spirit aspects of life will be downplayed, or they will be explained in culturally encoded ways that incorporate science and a rationalized religion.[45] In a similar fashion, Lévy-Bruhl thought that attention to phenomena depended on a selective choice, controlled to a large extent by values given to them; these values are expressed in patterns of thought and behaviour (collective representations). Patterns of thought and behaviour differ between non-Western and Western thought—selective interests differ widely, as does the degree of attention paid to them.[46]

Alfred Schutz (1899–1959), an Austrian philosopher, was also influenced by William James's notion of a stream of consciousness. He developed the phenomenological philosophy of Edmund Husserl (1859–1938), who saw in phenomenology, in its broadest meaning, a philosophy of experience and the source of all knowledge. It was Schutz who associated James's stream of consciousness with multiple phenomenological realities.[47] A phenomenological approach to an understanding of spirits is to suspend all belief and try to understand the experience. The aim of phenomenology is to suspend all natural or traditional belief in truths to focus on experience and what is meant by experience. Pure experience or pure subjectivity is the result of a stream of inner experiences.

However, problems still arise through conceptualizing spiritual beings, energies or a spiritual other world. As we have already seen, a common underlying element of magic is the notion of an imperceptible force or essence, and phenomenology cannot provide the conceptual framework for understanding this: the phenomenological analysis of the subjective experience of everyday life 'refrains from any causal or genetic hypothesis, as well as from assertions about the ontological status of the phenomena analysed'.[48] Phenomenology values the experience of spirits but is limited because it does not give us tools to analyse the reality of spirits as a part of human knowledge. We will return to this issue in the next chapter.

## A DANCE OF INTEREACTING PARTS

The study of magic takes our parameters of knowledge into new areas that are as yet relatively unexamined. In this section I invite you to explore being an advocate. Notwithstanding the potential obstacles, let us entertain the view that during the experience of magic, spirits share a degree of corporeal materiality and possess mind. Accepting this proposition allows us to imagine that their minds—embodied in whatever form we might imagine, be it bird, spirit tooth or goddess—and ours can meet in a wider consciousness; or put another way, mind *and* matter have consciousness. The body, the mind and the whole ecosystem are linked within a metapattern. Connections are made in terms of the mind, or minds, sharing stories, 'whether ours or those of redwood forests and sea anemones'; the pattern created is a 'dance of interacting parts (only secondarily pegged down by physical limits)'.[49]

As we have seen, historically, since Descartes associated mind with individual human reasoning, mind has been located in the brain, but consciousness is not reducible to individual brain activity. We tend to see consciousness as a product of the brain, and the brain can be scientifically studied through scans and machines that record brainwaves. However, consciousness cannot be understood by examining the brain. Consider, for a moment, another proposition that the brain is not the originator of consciousness, as is so commonly supposed in Western cultures, but only a transmitter of the sense impressions and thought processes of individual and social life. Molecular biologists have tackled the unravelling of the chemistry of the living cell, but that information does not indicate how cells interact to give life on a global scale. If a martian were to explore an earthling's television set, it could construct complex lists of its components but would not discover anything about how to watch the programmes or what they mean to its viewers.[50] If *mind* is defined as the personal aspects of individual process, and *consciousness* as an intrinsic quality of the wider universe of which individual mind is but one part, then mind and consciousness are linked. If consciousness is wider than the individual human mind, then that mind might be shared with other beings. If we understand these other beings as spirits that have a different order of existence to the material dimension of reality or invisible, but nonetheless real, dimensions of material reality, then it is possible to take the view that these beings also have mind. The implications of this are that we need to see beyond a purely materialist explanation of life and consciousness to see wider patterns.

We are necessarily limited by our knowledge, but in terms of the mode of magical participation, it is possible, as an advocate, to overcome the anthropological dilemma of the reality of spirits by adopting an attitude of spiritual agnosticism, by not believing or disbelieving in their reality. It is possible to accept that people believe in spirits and to keep an open mind as to belief. When a person is in that part of her awareness, it makes no difference whatsoever if she believes in spirits, or if spirit communications are labelled as psychological—if they are explained as part of their own internal thought processes—or whether the person thinks that the entities with which she is communicating are independent of her and have a being of their own. Whilst participating in a magical aspect of consciousness, the question of belief is irrelevant: belief is not a necessary condition to communicate with an inspirited world.

In this view, humans create spirits in their imaginations. The subject of the imagination is a perennial one when discussing the reality of spirits. When I have led workshops and given talks on magical consciousness, people always ask whether their experience of spirit communication is 'just' their imagination. My answer is that the imagination is an important tool for expanding awareness—in terms of magical knowledge, it is a doorway into an expanded participatory awareness. In practice, what starts as the imagination develops into something else entirely, or at least, that is the experience—the experience *feels* different and brings a different, often surprising, perspective. The spirits are real when they inhabit a person's experience or when that person inhabits the spirits' experience, or when the person becomes a part of another awareness, or when that other awareness becomes a part of the person's awareness, as in the process of shape-shifting when boundaries become less discrete, allowing the transmission of insight and knowledge.

Researching magic over the years, I have adopted an orientation that can shift between the analytical mode required by anthropology to examine the social and psychological *effects* of magical experience on people's behaviour, on one hand, and the actual experience of magic, on the other. It might appear to some people that the two orientations of the analytical mode and the participatory, magical mode are mutually incompatible; however, in practice, I have found that it is entirely possible to accommodate both aspects within a broader stream of awarenesses of consciousness. We are capable of experiencing multiple sensory inputs and of acting accordingly. Both modes can be used to complement each other. Indeed, the bringing together of the two can be most creative and can provide real insight.

So the question of the reality or nonreality of spirits appears to be unreasonable. At worst, it legitimises a denial of the experience of magic, and at best, it is a distraction from the further examination of this aspect of human awareness. The best way forward to start to feel this aspect of consciousness is to take the phemenological perspective of acting 'as if'—to bracket disbelief—and simply *experience*. What is essential about magic is a participatory relationship with an inspirited world. Tuhami's marriage to 'A'isha Qandisha (outlined at the beginning of the chapter) represents just one relationship that connects mind in a wider pattern of consciousness.

## NOTES

1. Edith Turner, 'The Reality of Spirits', in Graham Harvey, ed., *Shamanism: A Reader* (London: Routledge, 2003), p. 146.
2. Lucien Lévy-Bruhl, *The Notebooks on Primitive Mentality*, P. Rivière, trans. (Oxford: Basil Blackwell, 1975), p. 56; cited in Roy Willis and Patrick Curry, *Astrology, Science and Culture: Pulling Down the Moon* (Oxford: Berg, 2004), p. 120.
3. Gregory Bateson, *Mind and Nature: A Necessary Unity* (London: Fontana, 1985), p. 141.

4. Vincent Crapanzano, *Portrait of a Moroccan* (Chicago: University of Chicago Press, 1980), pp. 15–22.

5. Epistemology, coming from the mid-nineteenth-century Greek *epistémé*, meaning 'knowledge', is a theory of knowledge—its methods, validity and scope justified belief, rather than opinion.

6. Crapanzano, *Portrait of a Moroccan*, pp. 7–8.

7. Crapanzano, *Portrait of a Moroccan*, p. 8.

8. Crapanzano, *Portrait of a Moroccan*, pp. ix–xi.

9. Turner, 'Reality of Spirits', p. 145.

10. See, in particular, Roy Willis, *Some Spirits Heal, Others Only Dance: A Journey into Human Selfhood in an African Village* (Oxford: Berg, 1999).

11. Victor Turner and Edward Bruner, eds, *The Anthropology of Experience* (Urbana: University of Illinois Press, 1986), p. 33.

12. See Michael Harner, *The Way of the Shaman* (San Francisco: Harper and Row, 1990).

13. Turner, 'Reality of Spirits', pp. 145–7.

14. Michael Harner, 'Discovering the Way', in Harvey, *Shamanism*, pp. 41, 55–6.

15. Michael Lambek, 'Afterword: Spirits and Their Histories', in Jeannette Marie Mageo and Alan Howard, eds, *Spirits in Culture, History, and Mind* (New York: Routledge, 1996), pp. 238–9.

16. Mageo and Howard, *Spirits in Culture*, p. 12.

17. Robert Lowie, *Primitive Religion* (New York: Liveright, 1970), 99–100; cited in Robert I. Levy, Jeannette Marie Mageo and Alan Howard, 'Gods, Spirits, and History: A Theoretical Perspective', in Mageo and Howard, *Spirits in Culture*, p. 12.

18. Lévy-Bruhl, *Notebooks on Primitive Mentality*, p. 56; cited in Willis and Curry, *Astrology, Science and Culture*, p. 120.

19. Edward Evan-Pritchard, *Theories of Primitive Religion* (Oxford: Clarendon Press, 1990), p. 25.

20. John Henry, *The Scientific Revolution and the Origins of Modern Science* (Basingstoke: Macmillan, 1997), p. 172.

21. Antoine Faivre, 'Speculations about Nature', in Lawrence E. Sullivan, ed., *Hidden Truths: Magic, Alchemy, and the Occult* (New York: Macmillan, 1989), p. 24.

22. Henry, *Scientific Revolution*, pp. 43–4.

23. John Henry, *Knowledge Is Power: How Magic, the Government and an Apocalyptic Vision Inspired Francis Bacon to Create Modern Science* (Cambridge: Icon Books, 2002), pp. 5, 64, 79.

24. Henry, *Scientific Revolution*, p. 42.

25. Henry, *Scientific Revolution*, p. 42.

26. Godfrey Vesey and Paul Foulkes, *Dictionary of Philosophy* (London: Collins, 1990), p. 98.

27. Nigel Rapport and Joanna Overing, *Social and Cultural Anthropology: The Key Concepts* (London: Routledge, 2000), p. 273.

28. Henry, *Scientific Revolution*, pp. 19–20.

29. Brian Morris, *Western Conceptions of the Individual* (Oxford: Berg, 1991), pp. 6–14.

30. Henry, *Scientific Revolution*, pp. 67–8, 75.

31. Henry, *Scientific Revolution*, p. 4.

32. Lawrence E. Sullivan, introduction to *Hidden Truths*, p. ix.

33. Robin Horton, 'Lévy-Bruhl, Durkheim and the Scientific Revolution', in Robin Horton and Ruth Finnegan, eds, *Modes of Thought* (London: Faber and Faber, 1973), p. 297.

34. Tanya Luhrmann, *Persuasions of the Witch's Craft: Ritual Magic and Witchcraft in Present-Day England* (Cambridge: Basil Blackwell, 1989), p. 7.

35. Luhrmann, *Persuasions of the Witch's Craft*, p. 13.

36. Luhrmann, *Persuasions of the Witch's Craft*, p. 11.

37. Luhrmann, *Persuasions of the Witch's Craft*, pp. 312–13.

38. Luhrmann, *Persuasions of the Witch's Craft*, p. 12.

39. Luhrmann, *Persuasions of the Witch's Craft*, p. 312.
40. Luhrmann, *Persuasions of the Witch's Craft*, p. 145.
41. Luhrmann, *Persuasions of the Witch's Craft*, p. 156.
42. William James, *Principles of Psychology* (New York: Dover, 1950), pp. 288–9.
43. Peter Pels, introduction to Birgit Meyer and Peter Pels, eds, *Magic and Modernity: Interfaces of Revelation and Concealment* (Stanford: Stanford University Press, 2003), p. 12.
44. Edward Evans-Pritchard, 'Lévy-Bruhl's Theory of Primitive Mentality', *Bulletin of the Faculty of Arts (Cairo)*, 2 (1934), pp. 1–36.
45. See Stanley Tambiah, *Magic, Science, Religion, and the Scope of Rationality* (Cambridge: Cambridge University Press, 1990), pp. 12–15.
46. Lucien Lévy-Bruhl, 'A Letter to E.E. Evans-Pritchard', *British Journal of Sociology*, 3 (1952), p. 123.
47. See 'Alfred Schutz', http://www.seop.leeds.ac.uk/entries/schutz/, accessed 16 March 2009.
48. Peter Berger and Thomas Luckmann, *The Social Construction of Reality: A Treatise on the Sociology of Knowledge* (London: Pelican, 1984), p. 34.
49. Gregory Bateson, *Steps to an Ecology of Mind* (Chicago: University of Chicago Press, 2000), p. 467; see also Susan Greenwood, *The Nature of Magic* (Oxford: Berg, 2005), p. 97.
50. Stanislav Grof, *The Holotropic Mind* (San Francisco: HarperCollins, 1999), p. xv.

## FURTHER READING

Bird-David, Nurit, 'Animism' Re-visited: Personhood, Environment, and Relational Epistemology. *Current Anthropology*, 40, pp. 67–79, 1999; reprinted in *Readings in Indigenous Religious*, Graham Harvey (Ed) London: Continuum, 2002, pp. 72–105.

Greenwood, Susan, 'The Otherworld', Chapter 2, *Magic, Witchcraft and the Otherworld*. Oxford: Berg, 2000, pp. 23–47.

Grof, Stanislav, *The Holotropic Mind*, San Francisco: HarperCollins, 1999.

Hume, Lynne, *Portals: Opening Doorways to Other Realities Through the Senses*. Oxford: Berg 2007, especially chapter 8 An Anatomy of Reality, pp. 137–164.

Noll, Richard, 'The Presence of Spirits in Magic and Madness', in Shirley Nicholson, ed., *Shamanism: An Expanded View of Reality*, Wheaton: Theosophy, 1987, pp. 47–61.

Turner, Edith, 'The Reality of Spirits', in Graham Harvey, ed., *Shamanism: A Reader*, London: Routledge, 2003.

Turner, Victor, and Edward Bruner, eds, *The Anthropology of Experience*, Urbana: University of Illinois Press, 1986.

Winzeler, Robert L., *Anthropology and Religion: What We Know, Think, and Question*, Lanham: Rowman and Littlefield, 2007, pp. 218–20.

Znamenski, Andrei A., *The Beauty of the Primitive: Shamanism and Western Imagination*, New York: Oxford University Press, 2007.

# 9 'NOT ONLY, BUT ALSO': A NEW ATTITUDE TOWARD SCIENCE

One of the biggest benefits of learning anthropology is the realization that there are many different social and cultural ways of ordering life. This can be challenging because it makes us question our assumptions about things we often take for granted, for example how we think about magic and science. So far, we have considered the differences between magic and science as two modes of thought to bring the experience of magic into theoretical focus. Magic has been seen as the antithesis of science. We have seen that magical participation and its language of *mythos*—being based on emotion and affective relationships and associations—is fundamentally different to the activity of scientific experimentation, measurement and verification, with its corresponding language of *logos*:

| Magic | Science |
|---|---|
| Participation | Causality |
| Analogic | Logic |
| Subjective | Objective |
| Emotion | Reason |
| *Mythos* | *Logos* |

Although the comparison has been a useful theoretical tool to tease out some of the complexities of magic obscured by a rationalistic anthropology, it is now in order to look beyond these restrictive conceptual categories for a more inclusive scientific model, one that incorporates differences and is summed up by my use of the expression 'not only, but also'.[1] This will further aid our understanding of the anthropology of magic.

Philosophical studies of science have shown how theories are never value-free. Scientific theories do not arise from a vacuum; they are always dependent on social, political and cultural situations of their time.[2] Indeed, it was German sociologist Max Weber (1864–1920) who observed that all forms of rationality, including science, are ultimately grounded in subjective values.[3] Science, like any other human activity, must be understood within its context, and we must question our own assumptions. What we experience as we grow up is so familiar to us that we think that everyone shares the same reality. As English anthropologist, psychologist and biologist Gregory Bateson (1904–1980) points out, we are so accustomed to the universe in which we live and to our puny methods of thinking about it that we can hardly see that it is.[4] We create the world that we perceive; we edit and select from the universe so that it conforms to our beliefs and our vision of order. Bateson's work will help us analyse the anthropology of magic[5].

We can see the manner in which we view the world as patterns of different types of knowledge. For example it can encompass phenomenology as the philosophy of experience explored in the previous chapter[6]. Each pattern is not understood as one particular truth, but rather, as aspects that each have their own truth elements and that each relate to each other.[7] The aim of this final chapter is to bring about a reconciliation of magic and science in a new attitude that recognizes all the characteristics of magical participation *and* causality, analogic *and* logic, as well as the subjective and the objective, emotion and reason, and *mythos* and *logos*, as patterns of relationships that include mind and body, individual and society, within a wider scientific framework.

## MULTIPLE WAYS OF KNOWING

Visualise a spider's web that stretches across different branches in a hedge at dawn; pearls of dew hang from its delicate strands, and each thread makes a connection to the whole. This web is a wonder of nature in itself, but it can also be used for envisioning a different type of science. The metaphor of a web can bring together such seemingly disparate branches of knowledge as science (*logos*) and magic (*mythos*) into a new pattern that includes both. The experience of magic has been swept under the carpet in anthropology. As we have seen, Evans-Pritchard admired Lévy-Bruhl but wrote his classic ethnography on the Azande to show the rationality of beliefs in witchcraft, in response to claims that magic was irrational thus leaving other interpretations of magic largely unexamined. The web metaphor allows the pioneering work of Lévy-Bruhl as well as the usual more causally based theories to be brought into analytical focus. The web metaphor forms an *ideal* for multiple ways of knowing, but above all, it fosters a new attitude to knowledge, one that helps us understand the experience of magic in much more depth. A new attitude is required, and here we turn to English anthropologist Geoffrey Samuel's *multimodal framework*.

While studying Tibetan Buddhism and its shamanic aspects, Samuel came to realize that a new theoretical framework was required to incorporate very different forms of knowledge.[8] Coming from a background in both physics and anthropology, Samuel aimed at reconciling the natural and social sciences. Samuel draws on anthropologist Clifford Geertz's use of the web metaphor in his well-known phrase that 'man is an animal suspended in webs of significance he himself has spun'.[9] Samuel notes that the web is neither purely individual, because once it is spun, it can take on a life of its own, nor purely social, because webs have individual spinners.[10] For Samuel, the web is a conceptual space in which all knowledges, including magic, have their existence. Webs can be handy things to think with—they can be used as metaphors to express a language of relationship that incorporates different forms of knowing.

A metaphor is something that is representative or symbolic of something else, the word *metaphor* coming from the late-fifteenth-century French *métaphore*, meaning 'to transfer'. The metaphors that are chosen are not important in themselves; what is crucial is the idea that different types of knowledge are incorporated. This includes both informal and nonscientific and formalized knowledge that has crystallized into law codes, bureaucratic organizations, scientific theories themselves and so on. These formalized aspects are important parts of social reality and act back upon the changing flux of informal knowledge: 'once they have been created, they have a certain stability but they are not eternal and in time dissolve back into the general flow of informal knowledge.'[11]

Samuel observes a shift in scientific paradigm from seeing knowledge as a mirror (in which the gradual discovery of laws mirrored reality) to viewing it as a map (in which certain aspects of the territory are represented, while others are ignored). In the latter conceptualization, different fields of human knowledge are recognized as having different theories,[12] and each is represented. Each emphasizes different aspects of a situation that is too complex to be encompassed by any one of them.

What Samuel is advocating is a movement away from some form of objective knowledge, a view taken by the Viennese philosopher of science Karl Popper (1902–1994), among others. Popper held that the ultimate result of the painstaking making, testing and falsifying of hypotheses would constitute objective knowledge. Samuel contests this, saying that this achievement was implicitly related to some distant future; today, philosophers of science view science as a matter of competing theoretical frameworks, theories and approaches, each with its own degree of truth content. The issue here is how to ascertain the relative merits of different theories. Samuel points out that any relativistic picture must include all aspects; however, this leads to problems due to different academic languages used. This does not worry some scientists, who work in different academic contexts and can use their own descriptions without risk of conflict, but this is not so much the case in the nexus discipline of anthropology, in which competing approaches often come together.[13]

This inclusive framework for a different understanding of science is not relativistic, but rather, reveals different forms of knowledge that can then be utilized according to their usefulness. Giving the example of the activity of the mind, Samuel asks whether it is electrical currents or chemical flows in the brain that can determine the mind. His answer is that the mind cannot be understood by a single explanation, but both approaches to understanding can be included in a broader conception. Philosophers and psychologists provide a variety of alternate theoretical languages for mental activity that cover the same domain—none are reducible and none are right or wrong. Samuel argues that any realistic picture should include all aspects, which can then be considered for their relative merits. It might be difficult to create bridges of communication between the varying disciplines, but the new scientific model can aid the process.

### A Dynamic Model

In an attempt to make the metaphor of a web more dynamic, Samuel employs another metaphor of a stream or river, the currents of which he imagines as a structure of many webs laid out on the two-dimensional surface across the flow.[14] The flow is symbolic of the passage of time, and it is theoretically possible to metaphorically cut the river at any point to see the dominant webs during that historical period. For example, if we divide the river to make the webs visible to the seventeenth century, we would see that ideas about magic were a central part of everyone's consciousness, but that the ideas of Francis Bacon were starting to have a significant impact on how natural philosophers were examining the world in terms of scientific methodology (Chapter 3); and if we came forward to the 1920s, when Evans-Pritchard was conducting his fieldwork among the Azande, for example, we would see different cultural understandings of magic expressed in their African context (Chapter 6).

One of the advantages of this dynamic model is that it enables a historical perspective, and this makes it possible to see how earlier generations have dealt with specific issues surrounding an understanding of the world. Using the river metaphor, we can travel back to a period of German Romanticism (1790–1815) during the eighteenth century, when the *Naturphilosophen* (philosophers of nature) were attempting to bring back a sense of spirit to empirical investigation, and this will give us yet again a different perspective on magic.

Taking a grasp of the concrete character of nonphysical reality through imagination, the *Naturphilosophen* sought to link God, man and the universe using experimentation on nature. They used an intuitive approach that strived to be rigorous regarding the reality that underlay data derived from observation.[15] The early Greek Pre-socratic philosophers of about 600–400 BC inspired the *Naturphilosophen*. The

Pre-socratics were interested in the theory of the universe as an ordered system,[16] but they took the divinity of nature for granted and saw a divine principle pervading all phenomena.[17] The *Naturphilosophen* adopted a nondualistic, intuitive approach (with no opposition between mind and matter, or subject and object) that was reliant on analogy and paradox in their imaginative quest to attain the secrets of the universe.[18] In short, they sought to return a sense of spirit to a world that had come to be seen as spiritless and mechanical.

The metaphor of a river with its transverse sections cut to show chronological time can help us locate specific alternative approaches to a scientific understanding of the universe. It was the investigative spirit of the *Naturphilosophen* that led Henri Bortoft, a contemporary philosopher of science influenced by the eighteenth-century German poet and scientist Johann Wolfgang von Goethe (1749–1832) and twentieth-century American physicist David Bohm (1917–1992), to explore an alternative imaginative and intuitive approach to science. We can see how Bortoft's work contributes to a holistic approach to science very much in tune with Samuel's multimodal framework. Goethe was a poet, playwright and natural philosopher who was a leading figure in the *Sturm und Drang*, a movement that celebrated the restless spirit and opposed the rationalism of the Enlightenment.[19] David Bohm, on the other hand, was a physicist who combined the Indian mystical philosophy of Jiddu Krishnamurti (1895–1986) with his own ideas about quantum mechanics to view thought—to include the body, what is felt and the whole social sharing of thoughts—as one process, a system of connected things or parts.[20] Science and magic, in the form of mystical thinking, are brought together.

Bortoft views the conventional analytical view of science as an expression of a style of thinking that has its own validity, but he points out that it does not have access to ultimate reality. Bortoft suggests a complementary, holistic approach that involves a shift of consciousness from the specialized analytical mode to a holistic mode. This holistic approach creates a shift from a discursive, verbal-intellectual mind, with an emphasis on distinction and separation, to a relationship gained through intuition. By contrast to the analytical mode, the holistic mode of consciousness is nonlinear, simultaneous and concerned with relationships, rather than discrete elements that are related; it can only be experienced on its own terms, and it involves seeing a phenomenon in depth. The change from analytical to holistic consciousness is not a change in the content of consciousness, but rather, a change in the *mode* of consciousness.

The holistic mode of consciousness is only partly visible to the senses; the complete phenomenon is visible only when there is a coalescence of what Bortoft calls sensory outsight with intuitive insight. This happens in two stages: the first concerns a plunging into sensory experience (away from the verbal-intellectual mind—and here Bortoft makes parallels with meditation and the withdrawal of attention from thinking and reinvesting it in perception); and the second is allowing the imagination, as 'an organ of holistic perception',[21] to see into a phenomenon in depth. This depth is a further dimension of the same phenomenon, not another world hidden behind the sensory world. This is what Bortoft calls an *organic vision*. The key to this process is the imagination. Bortoft says that the imagination can be developed in an active manner by getting it to work.[22]

How is this done? Firstly, it is important to slow down, according to Bortoft, to follow every detail of a plant, for example in the sensorial imagination, and create an image of what is seen in the mind as precisely as possible. For example you look at a leaf, and you create the shape of the leaf as precisely as possible in your mind by moving around the shape of the leaf, following every detail. You produce the shape as a whole phenomenon as an image in the mind.[23] This approach is phenomenological (see Chapter 8)—it lets things become manifest as they show themselves[24]—which was something that Jung explored through the free association of ideas. The imagination moves consciousness into another space, much as poet and artist William Blake, a contemporary of Goethe, saw the entire world in the imagination. The plant is seen as a dynamical movement. This approach lets things become manifest as they show themselves, without forcing categories on them.[25] Imagination gives access to intuitive insights.

Bortoft gives another example:

> if we watch a bird flying across the sky and put our attention into seeing fly-ing, instead of seeing a bird which flies (implying a separation between an entity, 'bird', and an action, 'flying', which it performs), we can experience this in the mode of dynamical simultaneity as one whole event. By plunging into seeing flying we find that our attention expands to experience this move-ment as one whole that is its own present moment.[26]

Attention expands, and we experience the movement of flying. A sense of what Bor-toft calls authentic wholeness comes from dwelling in the phenomenon, not replacing it with mathematical representation; intuitive knowledge is gained through contem-plation of the visible aspect of a being, and when this happens, we see a phenomenon in depth. Bortoft notes that in following Goethe's approach to scientific knowledge, a person finds that the wholeness of the phenomenon is intensive and that 'the experi-ence is one of entering into a dimension which is in the phenomenon, not behind or beyond it, but which is not visible at first'. The phenomenon is perceived through the mind, when the mind functions as an organ of perception, rather than the medium of logical thought.[27]

Here parallels may be drawn with the shamanic experiences I have recounted earlier in this work, in particular, my experience of transforming into an owl, as described in the introduction. At this point, we have come full circle. Through the magical imagi-nation, it is possible to have wholly other experience. The practical value of this is that it forces us to reconsider our parameters of knowledge. How can we investigate unknown regions of experience with mental tools that come from an inappropriate method of analysis? It makes no sense whatsoever to examine the unknown with theories that obscure the focus of study. Samuel views such a shamanic approach (as in my experience of transforming into an owl) as a pattern potentially present in all societies; a pattern amongst other modal states in the multimodal framework that brings together different theories, including phenomenological and analytic, to link the entire human ecosystem within a series of relationships.[28]

## Webs are Patterns, Patterns Connect

The web consists of varying modes of thought that can be imagined as patterns. To reconcile different types of knowledge, Samuel has built on Gregory Bateson's ideas about a 'flow of relatedness', the emphasis on patterns of relationship and connectedness.[29] Bateson was drawn to cybernetics, an intellectual movement of mathematicians, neuroscientists, social scientists and engineers concerned with different levels of description that they saw as patterns of communication.[30] In this section, we will explore how Bateson's ideas about mental maps can contribute to our wider, multiply-connected rhizomelike conception of science.

In *Mind and Nature: a Necessary Unity*, Bateson tried to understand an integrated world; he attempted to come to an understanding of the world by being in the world, and he sought to find a language that would describe this relationship. Thinking that logic was not suitable for the description of biological patterns, he turned to metaphor as the language of nature. Bateson looked at the nature of mental processes—of thought in the widest sense of the word; he looked at the relationship between thought and the material world, and the evolution of mental processes.[31]

Concerned with thoughts and ideas about the world, Bateson was interested in how the mind classifies and maps things through *ideation* (the term coming from *ideate*, 'to imagine and conceive ideas in the mind'[32]). Bateson thought that we construct mental maps and organize connections and differences between things in a familiar pattern, and he was always interested in how the patterns connected.[33] *Abduction*, on the other hand, was the process of recognizing such patterns in dreams, parable, allegory, the whole of science and the whole of religion.[34] Abduction was a process of reasoning that organized information through metaphor. As we saw earlier, a metaphor is a symbol that connects one type of thinking with another, and relates varying forms of knowledge.

This notion of abduction helps us understand science and magic as different patterns of knowledge and understanding in what I call a 'not only, but also' fashion. Bateson gives Newton's analysis of the solar system and the periodic table of the elements as two examples of ways of organizing information.[35] The following three verses of a poem called 'A Valediction: Forbidding Mourning', by John Donne (1572–1631), are an example of a different type of pattern:

If they be two, they two are so
As stiffe twin compasses are two;
Thy soule, the fixt foot, makes no show
To move, but doth if th' other doe.

And though it in the center sit,
Yet when the other far doth rome,
It leanes, and hearkens after it,
And growes erect, as that comes home.

Such wilt thou be to me, who must
Like th' other foot, obliquely runne.
They firmness draws my circle just,
And make me end where I begunne.[36]

This poem, which was written by Donne to his wife before he undertook a journey, likens a compass to the relationship between two lovers.[37] It represents the relationship of two parts as they unite and move apart: the two compass feet form a pattern of connection. The important point that Bateson is making is that all forms of knowledge are connective patterns for understanding the world. They are not reality in themselves, but rather, ways of knowing, expressing and explaining realities through metaphor.

| **Ideation** | **Abduction** |
|---|---|
| Construction of mental maps through ideas and imagination | Process of recognizing patterns as metaphors |

Abductive systems, for Bateson, were relationships based on the recognition of corresponding patterns of behaviour that made 'patterns connect'. The aim is to break down habitual ways of thinking in terms of magic or science. The following example will show how scientific and magical conceptions of participation can be incorporated within the multimodal framework.

## PARTICIPATION REVISITED

In a paper titled 'Lévy-Bruhl, Durkheim and the Scientific Revolution', Robin Horton highlights the differences of opinion regarding participation between founding sociologist Emile Durkheim and Lévy-Bruhl. Horton compares Lévy-Bruhl's *How Natives Think* (*Fonctions mentales*) with Durkheim's *The Elementary Forms of the Religious Life* (*Formes élémentaires*[38]), and he is interested in how Lévy-Bruhl's early work focuses on participation characterized by native mystical thinking. The two authors differed over their understanding and use of the concept of participation, and here lies the crux of the issue. For Lévy-Bruhl, participation was mystical, an 'exemplar of everything that was most opposed to science'; whereas Durkheim thought that participation was far from mystical and was at the core of all logical life.[39]

Durkheim claimed that participation was at the very core of scientific thought and was the basis for all higher thinking. For Durkheim, there was no conceptual dualism between science and religion; his oft-quoted phrase was 'between the logic of religious thought and the logic of science there is no abyss'.[40] Uniting heterogeneous terms—by saying, for example, that a man was a kangaroo or that the sun was a bird—was not essentially different from saying that heat was a movement or that light was a vibration of the ether. Both employed the notion of participation and concerned, for Durkheim, an identification of contraries. In science, criteria were chosen for different reasons, but the process of mind as it classified and systemized phenomena was the same:

In fact, Durkheim viewed scientific thought as a more perfected form of religious thought. For Durkheim, the moment that religion was born, the possibility of all higher forms of thought, including science, was also born. When people symbolized an all-powerful yet unobservable collective force, this was the starting point for rational thought. In his view, there was continuity between primitive religious thought and modern scientific thought; the only difference was in degree, rather than kind.[41] Durkheim dismissed any attempt to define religion in terms of the mysterious or the supernatural. Religious thought was the precursor of scientific thought—he thought that the logic was the same and that both classified phenomena.

For Durkheim, religion accounted for the regular march of the universe, the movement of stars, the rhythm of seasons and the growth of vegetation, rather than anything extraordinary or unforeseen.[42] In this way, Durkheim sought to set aside the veil of mythological imagination surrounding religion. The mystery that surrounded religion was wholly superficial and disappeared with a more painstaking observation. Religion translated the mythological imagination into an intelligible language that did not differ from that employed by science; the attempt was made by both to connect things with each other, to establish internal relations between them, to classify and to systematize.[43]

Horton has characterized what he calls Lévy-Bruhl's contrast/discontinuity schema, on one hand, with Durkheim's continuity/evolution schema, on the other.[44] Noting that both authors had similarities in approach, Horton points out commonalities in how they explored the distinctions between primitive and modern thinking, and the way that they agreed on the primacy of social determinants on all thought (collective representations were ideas that were shared by most members of the social group and were handed down through tradition). They were also in agreement that the impact of society on the individual was responsible for the distinctive features of primitive thought. Both saw the growth of individualism in society as the key to the evolutionary transition from primitive to modern thinking[45]:

| Participation | |
| --- | --- |
| **Lévy-Bruhl** | **Durkheim** |
| Contrast/discontinuity | Continuity/evolution |
| Mystical | Logical |
| Exemplar of everything opposed to science | Core of scientific thought |
| Primitive and modern thought are antithetical | Primitive and modern thought are two stages in a single evolutionary process; the latter develops out of the former |

Although for Durkheim, magic was a negative and private activity, opposed to public religion, we can consider magic alongside religion as magicoreligious thought in terms of spirit beings. It is this spirit dimension that becomes invisible through the notion that such beliefs are misplaced mysticism, both being subsumed to a form of classificatory scientific thinking. By reducing mystical thought to a form of logical thinking (in the Durkheimian sense that scientific thought is a more perfected form of religious thought), Horton's objective seems to have been to discredit magic as 'mystical participation'. He then proceeds on a theme initiated in his earlier writing that traditional religious thought is similar to scientific thought.

Arguing that African causal connections with witches or spirits have affinities with scientific causal thinking, Horton has contrasted the relatively open nature of modern scientific thought with the more closed nature of its traditional African counterpart.[46] Scientific thinking uses predictive schemes as theoretical models based on commonly approved criteria, according to the scientific method. African religious systems are the counterparts of these theoretical models, but they do not have any guiding body of criteria that would ensure their efficiency.[47] For Africans, theoretical explanations are expressed in personal idioms; ideas about witches or spirits are the equivalent to what science describes as atoms and molecules. Like science, African theories place things in a causal context that is broader than that provided by common sense. For example, when an affliction caused by spirits is identified by divination, a causal link is created that connects disturbed social relationships and the affliction.

Horton's advocating of the Durkheimian continuity/evolution schema over the Lévy-Bruhlian contrast/inversion schema incorporates religion into the 'same process of mind' as science. In other words, religion, like science, is concerned with the classification of phenomena. Horton castigates the contrast/inversion schema for its mystical conception of participation, and in so doing, he devalues the magical aspect of participation. Horton's dismissal of mystical participation echoes Lévi-Strauss's view of mythology as a language of *logos*, ultimately claiming that the basic structure of the human mind is logical, rather than mystical, as discussed in Chapter 5. However, participation cannot be owned by either interpretation; it is part of a creative process of human thought, and it might be directed in a variety of ways. Using the multimodal framework, participation can be understood in terms of different forms of knowledge that each give a particular perspective, neither being right nor wrong, or mystifying (confusing) or clarifying.

| Ideation | Abduction |
|---|---|
| 'Participation' | 1. Can be explained by scientific thought<br><br>2. Can be explained by mystical thought |

Let us now turn to some other examples of how the multimodal framework can be employed.


## 'NOT ONLY, BUT ALSO'

In this section, we will examine briefly some issues that we have encountered earlier in the book to see how 'not only, but also' can be understood. In Chapter 6, we saw how Evans-Pritchard's work in *Witchcraft, Oracles and Magic among the Azande* was important for demonstrating that magic, as a technique for dealing with witchcraft and sorcery through medicines, was part of a whole system of beliefs: Azande life was lived through a pattern of understandings about witchcraft, oracles and magic. Evans-Pritchard's view was that magic should not be understood in isolation from Azande notions of witchcraft and oracles, and that this complex of beliefs was both rational and social. However, witchcraft and witches, as conceived by the Azande, cannot really exist because they are not explicable within Evans-Pritchard's materially based frame of reference. Evans-Pritchard's discussions with Lévy-Bruhl led him to focus on the rational aspects of native thought and argue that Lévy-Bruhl had made natives more mystical than they really were in his exposition of mystical mentality.

It is possible, using Bateson's notion of abduction, to present both rational and mystical approaches to help explain Azande magic:

| Ideation | Abduction |
|---|---|
| Azande Beliefs about Witchcraft, Oracles and Magic | 1. Magic is a complex system of beliefs that is part of a rational social order<br><br>2. Magic is a complex system of beliefs experienced through psychic connections |

Abduction is the patterns we make in our minds to understand and explain a given phenomenon or set of beliefs (ideation), and the web is a metaphorical conceptual space where all the abductive patterns can be examined. This includes areas of experience that have been restricted due to the history of emphasis on rationality and reason. So the question of the reality of spirits, for example, can be seen as offering two possibilities: spirits do not exist in the pattern of rationality, the pattern of *logos*, but they do in the language of *mythos*:

| Ideation | Abduction |
|---|---|
| The Reality of Spirits | 1. Spirits do not exist (language of *logos*)<br><br>2. Spirits exist (language of *mythos*) |

The practical application of 'not only, but also', incorporating both approaches, can be seen using the example of healing. By contrast to Evans-Pritchard, Edith Turner (Chapter 7) has examined spirit reality as a mode of consciousness by becoming more involved; this is something that Evans-Pritchard left to his servant, foregoing the actual experience of undergoing spirit initiation by a witch-doctor himself. By contrast, Turner was invited to the ritual as a healer, so she was intimately part of the process. Her whole body participated in the healing ritual to extract a spirit tooth from a sick woman; whilst in an alternative state of consciousness, she 'saw with her own eyes' a large, grey blob emerging out of the back of the patient. Here the multimodal framework offers new possibilities for bringing together previously separate traditions of non-Western holistic and Western biomedical models of healing. Both have advantages: the former for their integration of spirit with psychology, social dimensions and herbal medicine; and the latter in terms of their development of pharmacology and medical interventionist techniques. A new, more open attitude on the part of Western medical authorities could bring positive changes to how medicine is practised. In terms of magical consciousness, Western drugs, for example, could be interpreted as healing spirits in an internal battle with the spirits of sickness, such as described in my own Romani gypsy healing ritual in Chapter 7:

| Ideation | Abduction |
|----------|-----------|
| Healing | 1. Western biomedical model |
| | 2. Psycho-spiritual-social integration |

These examples of how the multimodal framework could be used to incorporate magical knowledge are necessarily brief, but they show how a new attitude of seeing ideas and beliefs and their metaphorical explanatory theories are patterns of knowledge that we make both individually (informally) and socially (formally).

The very fact that we all have the potential capability for magical consciousness means that this orientation of human experience must be incorporated into the wider picture. It opens up the imagination in a manner previously unrealized. As French philosopher Jean-Paul Sartre put it, 'Imagination is an activity in which human individuals are always engaged; and it is through their imagination that individuals create and recreate the essence of their being, making themselves what they were, are and will become.'[48] Imagination has a power which enables individuals to escape being swallowed up by a given reality, and it allows them to go beyond a certain situation, a set of circumstances and the status quo. Imagination gives the human world an intrinsically dynamic order which self-conscious individuals are continually in the process of forming and designing.[49] We can make a shift from examining magic only through its sociological or psychological effects, or solely as a logical classificatory mode of thinking akin to the older conceptualization of science, to a highly specific human mode of mind. The experience of magic must come in from the cold and take its rightful place within wider 'not only, but also' schemes of anthropological analysis.

## NOTES

1. When I am teaching this model to students, I often explain it as the 'have your cake and eat it philosophy'; this helps them to remember the most important part of the idea, and they always find it amusing!

2. Geoffrey Samuel, *Mind, Body and Culture* (Cambridge: Cambridge University Press, 1990), p. 22.

3. See Stanley Tambiah, *Magic, Science, Religion, and the Scope of Rationality* (Cambridge: Cambridge University Press, 1991), p. 153.

4. Gregory Bateson, *Mind and Nature: A Necessary Unity* (New York: Bantam, 1988), p. 153.

5. Nigel Rapport and Joanna Overing, *Social and Cultural Anthropology: The Key Concepts* (London: Routledge, 2000), p. 105.

6. See Samuel, *Mind, Body and Culture*, pp. 3–4, 30–2, 44–5.

7. Samuel, *Mind, Body and Culture*, p. 58.

8. Geoffrey Samuel, personal communication, 8th October 1996; Geoffrey Samuel, *Civilized Shamans: Buddhism in Tibetan Societies* (Washington, DC: Smithsonian Institution Press, 1993), p. vii.

9. Samuel, *Mind, Body and Culture*, p. 11.

10. Samuel, *Mind, Body and Culture*, notes the work of Bob Scholte, 'Comment on Paul Shankman's "The Thick and the Thin: on the Interpretive Theoretical Program of Clifford Geertz"?', *Current Anthropology*, 25 (1984), pp. 540–2, who wrote that in state societies, only a select few do the actual spinning, and the majority are caught.

11. Samuel, *Mind, Body and Culture*, p. 6.

12. Samuel, *Mind, Body and Culture*, p. 21.

13. Samuel, *Mind, Body and Culture*, pp. 18–19.

14. Samuel, *Mind, Body and Culture*, pp. 11–12.

15. Antoine Faivre, 'Speculations about Nature', in Lawrence Sullivan, ed., *Hidden Truths* (New York: Macmillan, 1989), p. 24.

16. G. Vesey and P. Foulkes, *Dictionary of Philosophy* (Glasgow: HarperCollins, 1990), p. 230.

17. Tambiah, *Magic, Science, Religion*, p. 11.

18. Faivre, 'Speculations about Nature', pp. 24–5.

19. 'Johann Wolfgang von Geothe (1749–1832)', http://kirjasto.sci.fi/goethe.htm, accessed 26 March 2009.

20. See 'David Bohm', http://twm.co.nz/Bohm.html, accessed 26 March 2009.

21. Henri Bortoft, 'Imagination Becomes an Organ of Perception', conversation with Claus Otto Scharmer (14 July 1999), http://unjobs.org/authors/henri-bortoft, accessed 26 March 2009.

22. Bortoft, 'Imagination Becomes an Organ'.

23. Bortoft, 'Imagination Becomes an Organ'.

24. See Henri Bortoft, *The Wholeness of Nature* (London: Floris, 1996), pp. 26, 62–71, 290.

25. Bortoft, *Wholeness of Nature*, pp. 26, 62–71, 290.

26. Bortoft, *Wholeness of Nature*, p. 64.

27. Bortoft, *Wholeness of Nature*, p. 21.

28. Samuel, *Mind, Body and Culture*, pp. 148, 152.

29. Samuel, *Mind, Body and Culture*, p. 55.

30. Fritjof Capra, *The Web of Life: A New Scientific Understanding of Living Systems* (New York: Anchor Books, 1996), p. 51.

31. Bateson, *Mind and Nature*. Bateson thought that evolution was *stochastic* (able to achieve novelty by a combination of random and selective processes).

32. *The Concise Oxford Dictionary* (Oxford: Oxford University Press, 1974).

33. Bateson, *Mind and Nature*, p. 153.

34. Bateson, *Mind and Nature*.

35. Rapport and Overing, *Social and Cultural Anthropology*, pp. 106–7.
36. Bateson, *Mind and Nature*, p. 140.
37. 'A Valediction: Forbidding Mourning', http://lardcave.net/hsc/2eng-donne-valediction-comments. html, accessed 26 March 2009.
38. Durkheim himself reviewed Lévy-Bruhl's *Fonctions mentales* in *L'Année Sociologique*, 12 (1913), pp. 33–7.
39. Robin Horton, 'Lévy-Bruhl, Durkheim and the Scientific Revolution', in Robin Horton and Ruth Finnegan, eds, *Modes of Thought* (London: Faber and Faber, 1973), p. 268.
40. Emile Durkheim, *The Elementary Forms of the Religious Life*, trans. John Swain (London: Allen and Unwin, 1915), p. 239.
41. Horton, 'Lévy-Bruhl, Durkheim and the Scientific Revolution', pp. 260–2.
42. Horton, 'Lévy-Bruhl, Durkheim and the Scientific Revolution', pp. 264–6.
43. Durkheim, *The Elementary Forms of the Religious Life*, p. 429; cited in Horton, 'Lévy-Bruhl, Durkheim and the Scientific Revolution', p. 264.
44. Horton, 'Lévy-Bruhl, Durkheim and the Scientific Revolution', p. 270, notes that Durkheim's continuity/evolution schema was the main thesis of his work; it does include a contrast/inversion aspect in his notion of the sacred/profane.
45. Horton, 'Lévy-Bruhl, Durkheim and the Scientific Revolution', pp. 267–9.
46. Robin Horton, 'African Traditional Thought and Western Science', *Africa*, 37 (1967), pp. 1–2; and Bryan Wilson, ed., *Rationality* (Oxford: Blackwell, 1970).
47. Robin Horton, 'Ritual Man in Africa', in William A. Lessa and Evon Z. Vogt, eds, *Reader in Comparative Religion: An Anthropological Approach*, 4th ed. (New York: Harper and Row, 1979), p. 251.
48. Jean-Paul Sartre, *The Psychology of Imagination* (New York: Citadel, 1972), p. XX.
49. Rapport and Overing, *Social and Cultural Anthropology*, pp. 4–5.

## FURTHER READING

Bateson, Gregory, *Ecology of Mind, Mind-ing Ecology.* http://www.oikos.org/baten.htm (accessed 13 september 2009).

Capra, Fritjof, 'The Logic of the Mind', in *The Web of Life: A New Scientific Understanding of Living Systems*, New York: Anchor Books, 1996, pp. 51–71.

Rapport, Nigel, and Joanna Overing. 'Cybernetics' in *Social and Cultural Anthropology: The Key Concepts*, Routledge, 2000, pp. 102–115.

Samuel, Geoffrey, *Mind, Body and Culture*, Cambridge: Cambridge University Press, 1990, esp. Chapters 1, 9 and 10.

# INDEX

communicating with spirit and, 139–41
contemporary example of, 29–31
dead and, 34
dreams and, 33
explanation of, 153–5
key features of, 31
as key to understanding magic, 29, 123
Lévy-Bruhl's definition, 11
Lévy-Bruhl's examples of, 25, 32–5
Lévi-Strauss and, 78
Morocco and, 36–7
Plato and, 39–41
shamans and, 29, 33–4, 38–9
spirit horse and, 70–2
stories and, 31–2, 38–9
vision quest and, 37–8
witches and, 34
phenomenology, 139, 146, 150–1
Plato
archetypes and, 41, 83
Divination and, 113
Eliade and, 40–1
humans and, 43n12
participation and, 39–41
Pythagorus and, 39
rationalist tradition and, 39–40
Popper, Karl, 147
pre-Socratic philosophers, 148–9

rationalism, 5, 9, 39–40, 105, 107, 135–7, 137–8

Sacks, Oliver, 63–5
Samuel, Geoffrey, 55, 147–51
Sartre, Jean-Paul, 157
science
analogy and, 54, 78
Cartesian legacy, 136
comparison with magic, 145
Descartes, 135–7
Durkheim and, 153–5
evolutionary ideas and, 49–50, 98, 133–4
healing and, 114
knowledge and, 12
myths as precursor to, 78
natural philosophy and, 134–5, 148–9
as paradigm, 147
positivism, 137–8
rationality and, 98, 134–5

Scientific Revolution, 134–5, 153
semiology and, 79
spirits and, 125
threats to, 131
scientific method, 7–8, 14n18
historical development of, 50–2, 134–5
neuroanthropology and, 63–5
shamanism, 65–7, 70, 118, 123–4
soul
animism and, 133
Descartes and, 136
healing and, 114, 116, 119–21
spirit
abduction and, 156
consciousness and, 139–41
definitions of, 132–3
Western assumptions of, 133–4
spirit worlds
abduction, 156
anthropological problems with, 8, 12, 131
communication with, 140
healing and, 114
reality of, 134
threat to science, 125, 131
structural linguistics, 179
Sturluson, Snorri, 11, 83, 91n25, 89
sympathetic magic
contagious magic and, 47–9
Frazer and, 45–52
homeopathic magic and, 47–8
natural philosophy and, 134
psychological experiments, 45–6

Tambiah, Stanley Jeyaraja, 11
biography, 53
persuasive analogy and, 53–6
tantric deity, 55, 147
tarot, 111–13, 138
Tedlock, Barbara 123
Turner, Edith, 121–3, 129, 131–2, 156

witchcraft
African, 2, 97–107, 155
European, 2–3
participation and, 34
studies of, 10
witch-doctors and, 3–4, 99–100, 102